Seize the Baton

RICHARD WEBSTER

William Carey Library
PASADENA • CALIFORNIA

Published & Distributed by:
William Carey Publishers
P.O. Box 40129
Pasadena, CA 91114

Cover Design: D.M. Battermann, R&D Design Services
Book Design & Layout: D.M. Battermann, R&D Design Services
Print Production: FTS Copy Service // Fuller Seminary Press

Contents

CHAPTER 1

From Chemist to Missionary

I sit here, up on the fourth floor of the Cardiac Intensive Care Unit in St. Joseph's Hospital, following my quadruple by-pass heart surgery. I will soon be seventy-eight years old. I look down at the orderly flow of traffic along Main Street, where it has been gliding along for over sixty years. Now the light turns yellow. The cars all slow to a stop. Then it turns red. The drivers wait patiently, staring blankly at the same buildings and signs they have seen a hundred times before. The light changes to green, and they all move on.

As pastor Ray Ortlund used to say, "Most people, even Christians, proceed through life like sheep, with heads down, just passing along from one tuft of grass to the next."

I began in that kind of pattern myself. My parents, though poor during the Depression of the Thirties, were honest, hard-working people who did their best to make proper provision for their five children. I admire them greatly for all the love and self-sacrifice they poured out on us. My father had to leave school before he finished the fourth grade to help support his widowed mother and younger brother. He never had an easy life.

When I graduated from high school, it was naturally expected I would get a job and begin the same pattern of "moving from one tuft of grass to the next" like those around me. In fact that was the extent of my own expectations. But one of my classmates had decided to enroll in Fullerton Junior College, just twenty minutes away in the next town. His father had bought him a nice little used car to drive there, and he urged me to join him in this venture. My parents were not particularly opposed to the idea, so we set out together. Both of us were interested in math and science, and I developed a particular fascination for chemistry.

After completing those two years, I got a job as a control chemist for the Filtrol Corporation in Los Angeles. This meant a one hour drive back and forth each day, and a rotating shift which was not very pleasant. But after only a year a surprising development took place.

Out of the blue, I received a letter from a Christian friend about my age – Dick Rowland — a chance acquaintance I had met only once or twice some time before. He was studying in the College of Chemistry at UC Berkeley, and strongly urged me to come up and join him. At first this sounded like a pipe dream to me, a small town country boy. With a measure of trepidation I tried to dismiss the thought. However I had done well in chemistry in Junior College, receiving the only A+ the professor had ever given. So the idea of further study was hard to put completely out of my mind.

Finally I sent a reluctant reply to my friend Dick, at the same time making a sort of deal with the Lord. If Dick wrote back and pursued the proposal, even inviting me to live with him, I would seriously consider the possibility. Sure enough! Here came a glowing letter, overriding all my reservations. In fact he excitedly announced he had located a room in the Christian Fellowship Hall right across from campus, for the two of us!

This facility was a dorm and meeting place for one of the fine Christian groups on campus. A couple dozen girls lived on the second and third floors; they were dubbed the "Upper Crust". A dozen fellows lived below the meeting hall, and they were called the "Basement Bums." Well, the Lord engineered it all, and I finally arrived at Berkeley, enrolled in the College of Chemistry, and along with my friend became a "basement bum" ready to begin university life. Surely for a hayseed like me, it was as if I had been transported to the planet Mars.

Still More New Developments

My new roommate Dick was quite outgoing and knew all the places to go and things to do in the Bay area. One of the first items on his agenda was to take me to a different church every Sunday and introduce me to his friends in each place.

After several months of this, we traveled to a small church out on the outskirts of Oakland. The pastor and his wife were very friendly and invited us to stay with them for lunch. About the middle of the afternoon, as we were chatting in their living room with background music on the radio, the announcer broke in with an announcement. "The Japanese air force has attacked and destroyed most of our U.S. naval vessels at Pearl Harbor. The President of the United States has declared war on Japan, and his declaration will be ratified by both houses of Congress tomorrow morning."

This development immediately changed the tone of life for every person in our nation. In short order eleven and a half million of our finest young men were drafted into the military forces. Almost every business began handling war contracts. Gasoline, certain foods, and a number of hardware items were rationed. All of life took on a wartime mentality.

Due to stepped up summer courses, in less than two years I finished my under-graduate work at the University, and was offered a position doing chemical research for the Manhattan Project right there on campus. The College of Chemistry had been granted several government contracts. In fact, the offer was even more enticing since I would be allowed to carry on graduate work at the same time. This was too good to let pass, so I accepted.

I was still able to live in the Christian Fellowship Center and attend their meetings. I might add that by this time I had begun to cast a glance at some of the attractive young ladies of the "Upper Crust." There was one in particular whom I admired the most, for she had a radiant personality, was a spiritual leader, and was loved by everyone. But I discovered a serious problem. She was planning to be a missionary to China, convinced that the Lord had definitely "called" her to that work.

I knew nothing about missionaries or their work. I had heard a time or two about such people who preached to the Hot-n-tots of Africa, or to some group of Eskimos up in Alaska. But such a career seemed as far removed from a university student as the East from the West. Yet this young lady seemed so sure of her "calling" that I dared not take even the first steps of trying to get acquainted with her.

The Sky Falls In

One evening the Fellowship group invited a missionary to come speak to us. I don't remember much of the content of his message, but I will never forget his conclusion. As he finished he said he would like to leave three questions with us, and he hoped each of us would give them serious consideration.

Question #1 was, "Do you consider yourself to be a *disciple* of Jesus Christ?" My answer was a firm yes. Question #2 was, "Would you agree that the Lord Jesus gave a commission to His disciples to take His gospel message 'to the ends of the earth'?" Yes, though I had never made a study of His commission, I had somewhere read these words in the scriptures. Question #3 was, "What are you going to do about it?"

I was so overcome by this simple, straight-forward line of reasoning that I immediately left the meeting hall, returned to my room, climbed into bed, pulled all the proverbial covers over my head, and tried to go to sleep. But of course sleep would not come. I tossed and turned until three o'clock in the morning, going over and over those three questions, trying desperately to find a loophole. But I could find no way out! Neither angry or rebellious, I was stunned and confused. Finally, at three a.m. I got out of bed, knelt down and told the Lord that although I had no idea where this all might lead, I was willing to follow whatever plan He had for me. Crawling back into bed, I fell into a deep, peaceful sleep.

The next morning I stood in the middle of my room and began to evaluate the happenings of the night before. I in no way doubted or questioned my commitment. That was clear and firm. But I was in a big quandary as to what I should do next. If one were to "do something about it", what would he do? The only thing I could think of was that if a person were to prepare himself for some phase of missionary work, he probably ought to study in a seminary. But I knew nothing about seminaries. I did remember that a fellow student in our group had been planning for some time to study for the ministry, so the next time I saw him I asked if he knew anything about seminaries. He replied that he had been collecting seminary catalogues for some time, and would be glad to bring them all over for me to look at. Soon after, he arrived with a stack of catalogues about six inches high.

I began to look these over, but they were all "Greek" to me, and I had no way of evaluating one against another. Then I thought of an idea. I figured that our Christian Fellowship sponsor would probably know something about seminaries, so I took the whole stack to him and asked him to look them over and suggest which would be most suitable. In a few days I saw him again, and he had picked out three.

So I sat down and wrote three letters, sharing a bit about my background, and sent them off. In a few days I had a reply from one of them, turning me down flat. They felt that since my study in college had been strictly in chemistry, and my decision to become a missionary was so sudden, that I was just a fly-by-night, and they were not prepared to give time to work with such an unsuitable person.

This did cause me to wonder if I was moving too fast maybe I should slow down a bit. To this day I have still not heard from the second school. But the third one offered me a warm, hearty welcome. In fact the registrar of that school, Dr. Laird Harris, had originally been a chemist himself!

Barriers Melt

Things were still not smooth sailing. I learned that in order to leave my research position, I must get a release from the War Manpower Commission. Several friends assured me that this would be impossible, since my only reason for seeking a release was to go to a seminary. Actually I would have been quite happy to just continue with my chemical research and forget any plans for seminary and missionary work. But I had no peace in my heart until I at least went down to the War Manpower Commission and asked for an application. They informed me that my papers would need to be signed by the head of the research project. I knew something about this professor and that he was definitely not a Christian. But when I approached him about the matter, he was very gracious and after a moment's thought said he would sign my request for release.

There remained one more sizable hurdle. How was I to get to this seminary which had accepted me? It was on the East Coast, and I was on the West Coast. All trains and planes had been taken over by the military. I had an old car, but gasoline was rationed so tightly that each person could receive only enough coupons per month for a few short trips around town.

There were offices where one could go to apply for extra gas coupons in cases of dire emergency, but these were of help only under very pressing need. Again I had no peace in my heart until I went down and submitted a request. When I arrived at the office the place was empty. Only one man sat at a desk in a corner of the room. At first he was polite and asked if he could help me. But when I explained that I needed enough gas coupons to travel three thousand miles across the

States to enter seminary, he lost his composure. He reminded me that we were at war, that we all must sacrifice for our country, and that his office was no place for foolish talk. I quickly apologized and turned to walk out. As I approached the door his voice reached me: "I must inform you" he added, "that I have to allow you to fill out a written application to be submitted to the Ration Board which meets every Tuesday night. But I assure you that it will do no good – it will only be a waste of your time." I decided then that since I was already there, I might as well go ahead and fill out the application, which I did.

After waiting a week, following the next Tuesday night I crept back into the "lion's den," just to check on the response. Again the place was empty, with the same man sitting in the corner. But when he saw me, the strangest expression came over his face. "I don't know what happened! I can't figure it out!" he muttered, "But they granted you the whole lot!" He handed me a stack of gas coupons, enough for my 3,000 mile trip to seminary.

Now the stage had been set, and rather quickly another barrier began to melt away. That was my hesitation in developing a serious acquaintance with that attractive young lady who was heading to China. Since I myself hadn't yet any particular missionary destination in mind, China sounded as good as any other, and she seemed to be quite delighted with the progress of my move toward missions. In June of 1944 Lucille and I were married, and a few days later we left for Faith Seminary in Delaware. By that time, after all the Lord's' amazing confirmations, I was quite confident of my own "call" to be a missionary.

CHAPTER 2

And He Was There

At the very end of the Gospel of Matthew, when the Lord Jesus was sending forth His eleven disciples as His first band of missionaries to "make disciples of all nations", He concluded His charge with a very special promise: "Surely I am with you always, to the very end of the age." (Matt. 28:20) This pledge is clearly a part of His "Great Commission." Or to state it more specifically, it is a firm guarantee to those sent forth to be missionaries. It is a very essential guarantee, for they are moving into enemy territory to plant the kingdom of a new King. The enemy kingdom includes unseen forces who extend no welcome to those coming with a gospel which spells their undoing. So conflict and harassment are to be expected. We will be mentioning more of this in later chapters, but an initial introduction to such uncanny opposition and hostility is in order at the beginning of any book on missions.

Many missionaries have moving stories to tell of the Lord's unusual intervention in the throes of the enemy's counter currents, and our first term, on the mainland of China, was no exception. It was also filled with countless amazing manifestations of His "being there." In this chapter, as a tribute to His faithfulness, I will relate a few of those incidents. But first we need to fill in a bit of background.

Getting Underway

As we moved into the second year of seminary, World War II ended and we decided to begin our applications to the China Inland Mission. We were delighted to eventually be accepted and invited to their candidate school in Germantown, Philadelphia. It was scheduled for the summer immediately after my graduation from seminary.

This six week course gave us a brief introduction to the Chinese language, an elementary review of Chinese history, an orientation to the background and functioning of the CIM, plus a chance to get acquainted with the home staff. Then within about a month, we boarded the troop ship "Marine Bear" in San Francisco, along with our ten month old son Donny and a dozen other missionary candidates. Three weeks later we arrived in Shanghai.

We were put up at the mission headquarters for a few days, and then began our trip inland to the mission's language school in the city of Anking in Anhui province a few hundred miles inland. The first leg of the journey involved a ten hour train ride to Nanking, the former capitol of China, and then a three day voyage on a small over-crowded launch up the Yangtze River. This launch had two staterooms, each less than six feet square, with two narrow bunks on either side. These little "broom closets" were reserved for the missionary ladies. The rest of us were on the deck with about a hundred friendly Chinese people who were transporting odds and ends of their goods up the river.

As much as I appreciated that colorful journey, it was a great relief to be able to step off the little launch and to get moved into our one room quarters at the language school. By the time everyone had arrived, including several from other missions and other countries, there were fifty-two of us. Now we were ready to tackle an intensive six-month course, designed to give us the basic rudiments of reading, writing and speaking Chinese.

Our living conditions were simple. There was a makeshift water supply in a few areas. Dim yellow electric lighting came on in the evenings. There was of course no heat, no inside plumbing, no radios or English newspapers. Yet those months were some of the happiest of my life. I learned to love simple Chinese food, to enjoy fellowship with Chinese people, and the beginnings of how to "endure hardness as a good soldier of Jesus Christ."

As the six months came to a close, it was time for "designations." A couple of the mission authorities arrived from Shanghai, and one by one we were each appointed to that part of China where we would undertake our missionary work. Since Lucille and I had previously been keenly interested in student work, we were assigned to the college town of Chengtu, capitol of the province of Szechuan in the extreme west, close to the Tibetan border. Actually we would spend the first year or so in the smaller town of Leshan, a hundred miles south of Chengtu, learning the Szechuan dialect and the culture of the local people. During that year we were mentored by a senior missionary couple, John and Jean Lockhart.

In order to reach our destination, Lucille and little Donny, along with another mother and her two children traveled on up the Yangtze on a small steamer to

Hankow, and then caught a plane to Chengtu. Next it was a long, all day ride on a rickety bus south to our city of Leshan. I was sent back to Shanghai and joined a couple of our missionaries to help drive a large Dodge truck loaded with baggage all the way to Chunking (in Szechwan). That trip turned out to be a full month's adventure!

Across China by Truck

It was on this trip that I really began to see why the Lord Jesus gave that special promise of *His presence* to missionaries. We hadn't gone far before we were deluged with summer monsoon rains, and this slowed us down considerably. After traveling about one mile on pavement through the outskirts of Shanghai, from then on it was dirt roads all the way. We crossed over (or through) at least a hundred streams, and some of this maneuvering was extremely precarious. On one occasion the raft available to ferry us across turned out to be far too small for our heavily loaded truck, and we came dangerously near to seeing everything dumped into the river.

At another juncture the river was so swollen and moving so fast, that we were told the only way to get across was to run our truck up onto a flatcar at the nearby train station and wait for a locomotive to come along and pull us across over the train bridge. This we did, but the planking put up for our unloading gave way, and again the whole load was very nearly dumped as we tried to get our truck down off the flatcar.

We had been hoping to reach the mission station in the city of Changsha by a certain Friday evening, so we could spend the weekend with friends there. But due to rains we were not able to arrive until the following Saturday evening a week later. As we pulled into their compound, before we had even climbed down from the cab of the truck, they came out to greet us with the news: "It's surely good you didn't arrive any earlier! Thieves have been raiding what few vehicles there are in this town, and taking away the starters, generators and any other crucial removable parts." At last though, the police had caught up with them.

The next major city we pulled into was Nanchang. Just as we reached the outskirts of town, the brakes went out on our truck. After creeping along slowly until we located the missionary working there, we were able to stay with him for a couple of days. He at once informed us that we couldn't have had our mechanical problem in a better place, for the U.S. government had set up a well-equipped repair garage in that city to train Chinese mechanics. They fixed our brakes in short order.

The most alarming part of the trip by far however, was when we hit the section of the "Burma Road" coming north out of Kueiyang. This stretch is known as the range of the "seventy-two bends." It was the steepest, most frightening series of sharp horseshoe turns I have ever encountered. As we started up the very first climb, I had to put the truck into compound low, and still it ground to a stop. While considering what to do next, I held the brakes down tight to keep it from rolling backward, but it began to skid toward the edge of the cliff. I knew I had to do something fast, so I put it into its lowest gear again, and decided to "slip the clutch" which would give me the equivalent of one lower gear, and we finally began to move forward. We were all praying, and once again the Lord exhibited His mighty presence.

Finally we reached a slope which was a bit less steep, so we could return to normal power. But the entire run of those seventy-two bends was so treacherous that our nervous energy was exhausted, and we ended up as limp as rags. While driving along, again and again we saw numerous cars and trucks in the valleys below which had gone over the edge. And after reaching the summit, we realized we were only halfway through the ordeal! We still had to go down the other side, which was equally terrifying.

Truly the Lord's special promise to missionaries: "Lo, I am with you always," is tremendous in its value. His very presence often means the difference between extended life, and therefore extended missionary work, or the end of it all. Although on occasion He does lift one of His servants out of his missionary career and take him "home" to Himself, as a rule His "presence" means special protection from many unanticipated dangers.

Other Special Provisions

When we had first arrived at language school, the exchange rate was sixteen Chinese dollars to one U.S. dollar. But six months later, when we left language school, it had risen to twenty-four to one. After our one month truck trip it had gone up to thirty-two to one, then six months later it was one hundred to one. By that summer, when we were ready to leave for a vacation up in the nearby mountains, it was up to one hundred thousand to one. When it reached twelve million to one the government decided to start over. They printed a new kind of bills and pegged the exchange at twenty-five Chinese dollars to one U.S. dollar. They were determined to hold the rate at that figure.

Right at that time we were in a real bind financially. I had accumulated five hundred U.S. dollars in my account in Shanghai because I hadn't exchanged any of my U.S. money for some months. Everyone said there would soon come a jump from the twenty-five to one rate, so I was anxiously waiting for that increase. But I couldn't continue this delay much longer. I had to have some money! So I called our Shanghai headquarters on the city's one public phone, asking them to exchange my five hundred dollars into Chinese money and send it to me. They did so, and the very next day the new currency had already leaped to one hundred twenty-five to one. This meant I now had only one-fifth as much Chinese money as if I had waited one more day.

Naturally I felt very upset over this transaction, and really wondered why the Lord had allowed me to get caught that way. Then an older fellow missionary who was visiting us at the time began to notice how downcast I was, and asked me what was wrong. I explained, and he gave a very wise comment. He asked, "Whose money was that? Was it yours, or did it really belong to the Lord?" Of course I replied that it was the Lord's. "Well then," he said, "don't worry about it. If the Lord can afford to take a loss on it, that's up to Him."

That statement became a great comforting truth to me, and set me completely free from trying to operate according to the exchange rate. It was a much needed release, for that new currency in just a few months inflated even to the level of sixteen million to one.

This run-away inflation meant that paper money really wasn't worth anything. A whole suitcase full of ten thousand dollar Chinese bills would be worth about ten dollars U.S. At one time I remember sending a letter to Lucille from a neighboring village, and having to cover it with fifty-eight thousand dollars worth of stamps.

So people began to deal in rice or cloth or other solid commodities. Finally, merchants started bringing out their Mexican silver dollars, selling these as reliable tender. Early each morning people would gather in the city park to buy and sell these silver coins. But no two silver dollars were worth the same price. You had to ring each one. The higher the pitch the greater the value. Gradually we had to work our way through that period of the spiraling exchange market.

Another difficult testing which came upon us was a problem with little Donny's feet. Shortly after getting settled in Leshan, we began to notice his feet turning in and curling down, somewhat like a club foot condition. This continued to grow worse so that we and others became really concerned. Why would the Lord allow this to happen when we had come to this isolated place for the sake of His kingdom? Was this another attack from the enemy's kingdom?

As we became more earnest in our praying about the matter, the Lord vindicated the promise of His special presence in a marvelous way. One afternoon a young girl of about eight or nine who used to play with Donny came running into our courtyard and announced that a foreign doctor had come to town.

It was a most unusual story. We learned that a wealthy old man there in Leshan had become desperately ill. His sons decided they must send for a foreign doctor from the capitol city of Chengtu. When word reached the missionary hospital there in the "big city," they sent one of their doctors to come check out this case. He traveled non-stop by bus, truck and rickshaw as fast as he could get there. When he arrived and examined his patient, he determined that immediate surgery was required. So they laid the old man on the kitchen table; the doctor sterilized his instruments and was about to begin. But by that time the sons were terrified by the sight of all the knives and other instruments, and they absolutely forbade the surgery to proceed.

Meanwhile the little girl had learned about this development and thought that perhaps we could persuade the foreign doctor to come to our house and look at Donny's feet. He was quite willing to do this, especially since the main purpose of his trip had fallen through.

As we talked with him we learned that he had just arrived in West China from Canada, and that for the past three years he had been doing research on the deformities of children's feet! He showed us exactly what to do to treat the condition, and today Donny's feet are perfectly normal.

Communist Takeover

After we had been in Leshan a year or so, the Communists, who had already occupied most of the northern half of China, managed to cross the Yangtze River and enter the southern half of the country. They first took over the major cities in the east, along the coast. Then they began a steady, progressive march west. This meant of course for most of the population a nerve-racking wait, followed by a period of even greater anxiety and uncertainty as the troops *arrived* in each region. However, the China Inland Mission leaders had decided their missionaries would not flee, but just wait and see what developed.

As this "invincible" army drew close and began to penetrate our province of Szechwan, it was just the time when our family needed to make a trip to the mission hospital in Chengtu for the birth of Donny's little sister. The countryside was already in the throes of turmoil, so the journey was fraught with plenty of hazards.

On the night before the surgery, the city of Chengtu was surrounded by the new Red troops, and the blasts of cannon fire sounded all around us through the night. When morning arrived, I went out to find a rickshaw to take Lucille to the hospital, but there was not a soul in sight. The streets were deserted. Usually in the early mornings there would be hordes of people milling around doing their shopping or on their way to work. But not that morning!

I eventually located a friend who knew a rickshaw man, and he very reluctantly agreed to help us if we paid him a fancy price. So we started out! As we moved through the main street of town, we came into a once-in-a-lifetime situation. The Communist troops were marching into the city on one side of the road, and the Nationalist soldiers were marching out of the city on the other side. And we were moving right down the middle of the road between them! Once again, how reassuring it was to know the Lord's very special presence.

Arriving at the hospital, we saw that it was already filling up with wounded soldiers. Stretchers were even filling the passageways. But the surgery was performed, and a baby girl was brought safely into the world. Then mother and baby needed to be transferred somehow to a nearby missionary's home. How was that done? Mother Lucille was borne on a stretcher completely covered with a sheet (disguised as a corpse), and baby Dorothy followed, hidden in the midst of a bundle of laundry!

After a few weeks, we managed to acquire seats in one of those rickety busses for the trip back to Leshan. When we arrived, our senior missionaries were very relieved to see us. They announced, "This is the first bus in weeks which has gotten through without being held up by bandits!"

Now we discovered that our house was occupied by Communist soldiers, so we had to move into an abandoned school building nearby. There we lived for a year and a half, until we were granted permission to leave the country.

The Pressure Increases

At first the Communist authorities gave everyone, including us foreigners, a warm offer of friendship, encouraging us all to carry on with our work and activities as usual. But this stance didn't last long. They soon began to round up the well-to-do landlords, any who had ever spoken out against the Communists and those who had had "too much" communication with Americans. This made it doubly hard for the church people, since the Communist regime is so anti-Christian to start with. We could soon see that our very presence was much more of a hindrance than a help to the Lord's flock, so before long we began application to leave the country, as did all the other missionaries in China.

However, it soon became evident that permission to leave was not all that readily forthcoming. It took us a full year and a hundred trips to the police office before our request was granted. It certainly appeared that they were prepared to give us a full course of harassment.

It wasn't long after the Communists' arrival that they began daily executions just outside the city wall, not far from where we were living. Every morning about nine a.m., a dozen or so "questionable characters" would be shot. Our language teacher was one of them, and a Christian doctor who lived next door very narrowly escaped. Deciding that his medical knowledge would be of value to them, they kept him in prison at night but busy tending their sick and wounded during the day. The downtown church was converted into a political library.

As the months wore on, little Donny finally became exasperated over the long delay in waiting for our exit visa. Finally one night as he was saying his prayers at bedtime, he called out to the Lord: "God, please give us that paper tomorrow!" And sure enough, the next morning we received notice that we could leave!

An Arduous Exit

We were given just three days to get our things packed into footlockers and to have those footlockers inspected. What an inspection it turned out to be! Each box was emptied and measured inside and out to make sure there were no false bottoms. Then a detailed list of the contents of each box was written on a slip of tissue paper. After re-packing, each lid was sealed with its tissue paper list. Most of our packing had been done long before, but it took nearly the whole three days allowed for the inspection process. Finally we were informed that we would be leaving the next morning. But would you believe it! The next morning when the inspectors arrived to check on the sealed boxes, all the seals had been torn off! We discovered that our little one-and-a-half year-old toddler Dorothy had wandered down the hall into that room and enjoyed herself peeling off those "papers".

I have rarely seen anyone so angry as the head inspector was that morning. He finally stomped out, declaring that he would have nothing further to do with those boxes and that we were up to our own resources to solve the problem. But just as he stomped out, another officer came in, who was very eager for us to be on our way so that he and his men could take over our quarters. I began to explain, but he quickly waved us on with the words, "Don't worry about it – just get those boxes out of here!"

Well, to make a long story short, those boxes were inspected nine more times on their way out of China. Gradually their most valuable contents were confiscated, so what was finally left wasn't worth very much.

All missionaries had to undergo a very thorough interrogation by the Communist authorities as they passed through Chungking (largest city in Szechwan) on their way out from west China. When the morning came for the Lockharts and ourselves to meet for this lengthy, grueling ordeal, everyone was praying earnestly for God's intervention, since I had worked for a time back at Berkeley on the Manhattan Project. The inquisition began with the Lockharts and certainly left no stone unturned. Next came Lucille's turn, and I had never seen her so emotionally spent as when her interview was over. So I was the final one. But an amazing thing happened! The officer in charge looked at the time, and since it was already twelve noon, they only asked me two simple questions and we were all dismissed.

In conclusion to this chapter, I want to finish with a grand assurance. If the Lord should ever call you to be a missionary, or if your role is to be that of praying for missionaries, always keep firmly in mind that He gave a definite, concrete promise specifically for those who go: *"Lo, I am with you always, to the very end of the age."* Do not fail to learn how to claim this truth and appropriate it every step of the way.

CHAPTER 3

Seeing God
At Work

After we had made our exit out of China (through Hong Kong), we returned to the U.S. for a period of recuperation. In a few weeks the mission asked us to work with Chinese students at my old alma mater, the University of California at Berkeley. This we did for a little more than a year, but then came a strong yearning to get back to the needy multitudes of Chinese overseas. Taiwan was the new stronghold of "Free China", and several missionaries had begun to enter this new field. As we sought the Lord's guidance about such a move, He began to open doors, and before long we found ourselves situated in the southern part of Taiwan in the city of Tainan. And this time we brought along a second little daughter, Darlene.

We hadn't been there long until two factors became clearly evident. First we were struck with the intensity of idol worship in Taiwan. There were Buddhist and Taoist temples everywhere. The people patronized these dark, fearsome centers with much more devotion than anything we had seen in mainland China. There had been a few temples here and there on the mainland, but most of them were frequented by only a few people, and after the Communists came all religious projects were closed down. But in Taiwan, not only were the temples flourishing, but idol-toting parades took to the streets regularly, with all their drums, gongs and flutes. Every heathen funeral of any size had a long, marching entourage of pious followers dressed in sackcloth, white gowns, or yellow priestly robes. Often loud music in minor keys would accompany these parades.

Superstitions abounded, holding the people tightly, and nearly every home had a large idol altar in the living room. This held the idols, candles, incense urns, ancestral tablets, and other paraphernalia. When pagan festivals came due, families would place a table in front of their home loaded with various food items offered to the gods. Each supported its incense sticks, and each family member would light his own stick and bow low in obeisance to the deities or their ancestors. In Taiwan we had a moving introduction to stark paganism.

The other factor which impressed us in Taiwan was in complete contrast to all this idolatry. That was a noticeable hunger for spiritual truth among the people. Not only were Christians eager for biblical teaching, but many non-Christians were quite ready to listen to a gospel presentation. Doubtless one reason for this was the destitution of the refugees from the mainland of China.

I was profoundly impressed with this zeal one day shortly after we arrived. I had been invited to speak at the Sunday morning service of a downtown church. But the night before, a heavy typhoon struck and much of the city was flooded. Our own house had a foot of water flowing through it downstairs.

Surely there would be no worship service that morning – I assumed everything would be canceled. Yet I had no peace of heart about not showing up. So I got dressed, rolled up my pant legs, got on my bicycle and pedaled downtown to the church. When I arrived, the first service had just finished and crowds of people were pouring out. Throngs were waiting outside for the second service at which I was to speak. How glad I was I had brought my Bible and notes along!

*Note: The picture now has drastically changed in Taiwan. While the material standard of living has steadily risen, the hunger for spiritual light has decreased proportionately.

God's Strategy Unfolds

Our God is assuredly a skilled strategist. In all our planning, how wise it is for us to give Him ample room to show us *His* way!

On one occasion, when the Lord Jesus was picturing Himself as the "Good Shepherd", He made the statement, "When He puts forth all His own, He goes ahead of them, and the sheep follow Him because they know His voice." (Jn. 10:4 NASB) This is a good verse for missionaries. It could be paraphrased: "When he sends forth His own messengers, the ones He has especially chosen, He goes ahead of them to work out the most effective strategy for their work. And they follow Him because they know His voice." How blessed is the missionary who has learned to detect and follow His Shepherd's voice.

When we first arrived in the city of Tainan, we had little idea of what we would be doing, and even less knowledge of how to begin. But the Lord soon began to unfold His plan. A lady missionary in that city had recently been invited to give English instruction to a dozen teachers in the College of Science and Engineering nearby. Since science was not her area, she asked if I would take the class. I was delighted and soon became a regular figure on campus.

Before long we learned that most of the students we met, whether college or high school, were eager to learn English. So we started a few classes with the Modern English Gospels as our text, repeating everything in both English and Chinese. Many students were hungry for spiritual truth, and one by one they began to turn to the Lord.

Then there came invitations to teach English Phonetics in other schools, both to college and high school, and these helped increase the attendance at our Bible classes. About this time I met a young Navigator missionary from another town, and he convinced me that I needed to give more attention to the follow-up of those turning to the Lord. Since the Navigators are specialists in discipling new converts, I asked him to give me some training. This he gladly did, and a whole new phase of missionary work opened up for me.

I began to set up weekly appointments for each new believer, to help them get started in daily devotions and other aspects of their life and service. This seemed to please the Lord, for the harvest began to increase beyond what I could handle. In fact I over-extended myself and came down with TB, which brought us back to the States for an early furlough.

After a year however, we were back in Taiwan and fresh winds were blowing. Student Bible classes of several kinds were now being carried on by missionaries in each of the main larger cities. We began to compare notes and share our experiences, and soon the Lord in an unusual way started to disclose the next step in *His* strategy.

One day out of the blue, we received a letter from Gwen Wong, a friend we hadn't seen in years. She was a Chinese classmate at UC Berkeley and attended the Christian Fellowship when we were there. She had been doing student work in the Philippines and wondered if she could come visit us. Of course we warmly welcomed her, and soon she arrived. We had good fellowship together, and she looked over the student work we had been doing.

Finally she mentioned that she felt the time had come for our work to take some steps forward. She pointed out that as long as everything centered around the missionary, things could not fully develop. The students needed to move from passive to active involvement. They needed to see the work as their own. The Christians of each campus should come together and do their own planning, praying, and outreach to their fellow students. Missionaries could speak by invitation, but the students were to take the reins and promote it themselves.

Since Gwen's work in the Philippines was now in the hands of local staff, she offered to come to Taiwan for a time and help get the work into this new orbit. We were glad to have her come, and during the next two years she served as a catalyst, helping bring the island's college and high school student work into an indigenous unit called Campus Evangelical Fellowship.

"Lengthen Your Cords"

At first it might appear that with Gwen's coming, we missionaries had worked ourselves out of a job. Actually, that should have been our goal from the be-

ginning. But it didn't quite turn out that way. There
were always plenty of invitations to speak to the various student groups and churches, while other things
in God's strategy took place as well.

Once a year we missionaries were to have thorough physical exams. So right in the midst of these
new developments in the student work, we took a day
off and traveled fifty miles south to the town of Pingtung
where there was a small mission hospital. After our
check-ups there, the following Saturday we received a
phone call from Dr. Berg asking us to come see her the
next morning. "But tomorrow is Sunday!" I replied.
"Your clinic is not open on Sunday." "Yes, but I need to
see you," she answered.

As we pulled up in front of her house, she took us
into her small living room and began to explain that
Lucille had a cancerous condition which was very serious. She needed to return immediately to the States
for treatment. Then in her own sweet way, Dr. Berg
(whose husband had been murdered on mainland
China years before) offered to share a portion of scripture with us before we left. She opened her Bible to
Isaiah 54 and began to read:

   "Enlarge the place of your tent,
    And let them stretch out the curtains of your dwelling;
    Do not spare;
    Lengthen your cords,
    And strengthen your stakes.
    For you shall expand to the right and to the left,
    And your descendants will inherit the nations,
    And make the desolate cities inhabited."

Then she prayed a beautiful prayer for us and bid
us goodbye. We were stunned as you can imagine,

but an unexplainable peace also came upon us. Then in a few days the Lord gave Lucille another portion of His Word from the next chapter of Isaiah:

"For My thoughts are not your thoughts
Nor are your ways My ways," says the Lord.
For us the heavens are higher than the earth,
So are My ways higher than your ways,
And My thoughts than your thoughts."(Is. 55: 8,9)

Lucille flew back to the States with our two daughters, whom she left with her parents, and entered the City of Hope hospital in Duarte, California. Don and I stayed on in Taiwan for the six months they were gone, and some amazing things happened during that period. Already we could see unfolding the fulfillment of those verses in Isaiah 54 and 55.

One afternoon a Christian Chinese businessman, a good friend of mine, asked me to go with him to the countryside to see a piece of land he had just bought. Needing a break, I went along. To reach the place, we walked a quarter mile through a beautiful wooded lane, finally arriving in a picturesque clearing by a small stream.

I was immediately taken with the spot and asked if we could bring a group of students there sometime for a little retreat. He was happy with the idea and even suggested we might put up a little shed to hold some cooking equipment. Then we could come for a day at a time, even regularly, and enjoy some cookouts.

When the students first visited this little "paradise", they were thrilled with it. They began to make plans to put up the small storage building. But this was only the beginning. We discovered that the Lord had more plans in mind. A couple of farmers who owned ad-

joining land were anxious to sell and offered their plots
at very reasonable prices. To confirm this property as
His gift to us, the Lord sent in some special gifts right
at that time. Then to cap it all off, when my businessman friend, who had purchased that original piece, saw
what the Lord was doing, he decided to donate that
section.

The treatments Lucille received at City of Hope were
without charge, and yet a number of churches and individuals kept sending in sizable gifts, which enabled
us to begin developing a full-scale camping facility.
Following the dormitories came a chapel, then a din-
ing hall, caretaker's quarters, basketball court, and
lovely landscaped areas. True, these buildings and their
furnishings were simple and plain because we wanted
to make the Lord's money go as far as possible. Yet
the students were ecstatic with what He had done.

Together we agreed on a name – Mount of Olives.
Not only were a few olive trees growing there, but back
in Bible times the Mount of Olives was where the Lord
often took His disciples for their spiritual retreats.

From the start, it was evident this was "holy ground",
and with joy we saw the blessing of the Lord come upon
it. During summer and winter vacations it was packed
with students attending retreats and camps. Some
camps were evangelistic and some were for training
Christians. On those grounds hundreds of young people
met the Lord, and scores who committed their lives to
Him there are now in full-time ministry.

After a rather prolonged battle with her cancer, the
Lord took Lucille home to be with Himself. But it
seemed that He had raised up the Mount of Olives as a
monument to "His higher ways" in her behalf. Lucille

had been not only a wonderful partner to me, but a tremendous asset to the work. She conducted a good number of Bible classes for the students, and led many of them to the Lord. As a counselor she brought much comfort to the endless stream of those who sought her out for her words of advice and wisdom.

Family Developments

About this time I was invited to join the faculty at Christ's College in the northwest of the Island. The two years spent there gave a rich opportunity to get involved in the lives of a whole new batch of students and to adjust to the changes that had come into my life. Our three children were enrolled in the missionary boarding school, Morrison Academy, in the city of Taichung at the center of the island. So for the next two years I lived pretty much alone. But I was able during that time not only to teach at the college, but to make regular trips to the Mount of Olives Camp to oversee new construction and expansion there. The camp grew during this period to several times its original capacity, and this physical growth was attended by great spiritual blessing as well. Hundreds of students turned to the Lord, and many of them are in full-time Christian service today.

In the Lord's time, my eyes became more and more attracted to a sparkling young missionary to students, Miss Florence Shires, who was helping Campus Fellowship in the north of the island. She had been trained under Gwen Wong, was a very effective worker, and everyone liked her. The Lord graciously helped develop a relationship between us, with the beautiful result that Flo and I were married on Valentine's Day in 1965.

We settled in Taichung, the second largest educa-

tional center of Taiwan. It had a dozen colleges and
universities and even more high schools. We were also
drawn to this city because our daughters could live at
home with us and still attend Morrison Academy. Don
had just returned to the States to enter Wheaton College, but Dorothy and Darlene readily accepted Flo as
their new mother, and that lovely affinity has continued to grow in its beauty to this day. Another element
which cemented our family's love all the more was the
Lord's gift to Flo and me of two little sons, Larry and
Sam. Yes, once again we have a happy, radiant family.

Flo had already been vitally involved in the student
work, and now she and I had the joy of working together as partners in it. She was often invited as a
speaker at the student meetings, and helped in the
training of the various student leaders. She was also
gifted as a counselor, and her training as a teacher
gave her special skills in other areas. Truly, a
missionary's partner often turns out to quite definitely
be his "better half." At the time of creation the Lord
made the statement that it was not good for man to
work alone. That truth is compounded many fold when
it comes to missionary work.

Also, at this time after serving for nine years as in-
dependent missionaries, we joined TEAM (The Evangelical Alliance Mission) and once more began to enjoy the blessings of belonging to a mission family.

Out to the Villages

Shortly after settling into the Campus Fellowship
program in Taichung, the Lord began nudging us to
renew an emphasis on missions. We knew that no
missionary has completed his work until he has im-
parted a vision for world outreach in the hearts of his

disciples. Whether planting a church or doing student work, he needs to help others catch the vision of the Great Commission and getting the gospel "to the ends of the earth."

At first we faced a real obstacle. There was no sending "mission" for the Chinese to join! Whereas in the U.S., young people have scores of mission boards to choose from, in Taiwan there was only one, and it had never really gotten off the ground. Our American and European mission boards were not set up to receive these Chinese students, so how could they really consider overseas ministry? Then the Lord showed us they didn't actually need to go overseas. True, there were churches in most of Taiwan's towns and cities, but many village areas were completely unreached.

The island of Taiwan is divided into fifteen counties, and each of these is divided into districts called "hsiang". Each hsiang contains twenty to forty villages. We began to look over the statistics and discovered that many of these hsiang with their dozens of villages had not even one church. Here was a totally unreached mission field right at our own back door! Heathen temples abounded and were very active, at least one in every village, but what a spiritual wilderness exists without the gospel.

Sunday afternoons we started taking teams of students out to lead outdoor Sunday Schools for the children. They responded, eagerly singing gospel choruses, memorizing scriptures, listening to Bible stories. But only a few of the adults would gather round to listen.

In the evenings we began to take teams out to show Christian movies. The farmers had finished their evening meal and quite enjoyed watching the movies.

Through these films we covered many villages, but it was only a beginning introduction to Christ, hardly penetrating into the distorted lives of these people.

We needed to make more of an impact, and this called for a greater commitment by the students. What about their summer and winter vacation times? Would they be willing to give a week to go and live in the villages, visiting the homes one by one and searching out those who would listen? Yes, a good number were willing, and the spiritual challenge the students themselves received was often the greatest benefit of all.

But they needed training, as this was no venture to be casually undertaken! So each time a gospel team went out, the first day was given to training. After that, each morning was set aside for prayer and heart preparation; then in the afternoons they went out to the people. In the evenings there was often a gospel meeting held in some central spot in the village.

The response to these efforts was varied. Good seed was sown and some villagers made valid decisions. But we knew the follow-up would be inadequate. After the week was over and the students went home, that was the end of that particular project. The next group would go to a different district. Surely though, the students themselves were deeply impacted. Their eyes had been opened to the desperate need for the Good News in these dark, pathetic regions.

After several years of taking gospel teams out, we began to pray and seek for long-term workers. Some of the students had graduated now, and a few others considered moving into one of these "hsiang" to live there, set up a church, and teach the people how to worship the true and living God. Step by step, the Village Gospel Mission was formed. Single workers and several married couples began to respond. It was not easy for any of them, and we learned many new lessons about spiritual warfare as they sought to enter these heathen strongholds. But our hearts were greatly encouraged as we "watched God work." This kind of thing holds high priority with our Father.

Now as I write this, there are six little churches functioning in six of these formerly unreached hsiang. The young Chinese workers are supported with funds and prayer by other fellow graduates who share the same vision, and I am sure the Lord is greatly pleased.

While this village outreach was going on, other opportunities also came to us. Flo was invited to teach Bible classes and prayer classes at Morrison Academy, the school for missionary children. And we found ourselves more and more involved in training and counseling younger missionaries and Chinese workers. Our speaking ministry also grew to include a good bit of sharing at retreats and conferences. So, in both English and Chinese, the Lord allowed us to encourage and give to others what He had so abundantly given to us. In the midst of the spiritual warfare He taught us marvelous lessons in prayer.* It has truly been an adventure to see His plan unfold.

*Worship & Warfare, by Dick & Flo Webster, is a Prayer Companion Guide based on using scripture in prayer. Tearing Down Strongholds, by Dick Webster, is written for the Christian worker facing the powers of darkness. The books are available:

1. in English from Wm. Carey Library; P.O. Box 40129; Pasadena, CA 91114. Tel 1-800-MISSION or (626) 798- 0819. Email: orders@wclbooks.com

2. in Chinese from: EFC Bookstore in El Monte; Tel. 1-800-888-7796 or (626) 307- 0030 Email: efccc@efccc.org or GLORY Bookstore in Monterey Park; Tel. 1-800-795-1985 or (626) 571-6769 Email: info@ccbookstore.com

CHAPTER 4

Our Father's Heartbeat

During several furloughs and recently in our three years of semi-retirement, we have visited a good number of churches across the country. We have discovered that for a majority of Christians in America, world missions has been a low priority in their thinking. In my own upbringing it was the same. Yet in the heart of our Father, missions hold a central position.

Since God is our *Father* and we are His *children, it follows logically* that our priorities and primary concerns should be the same as His. When we begin to check out His heartbeat in scripture, we soon see that taking the gospel of His love and redemption to the uttermost parts of this world stands at the top of His list.

His Eyes are Looking at the Whole World

Let us examine then, a few key references from scripture. Probably the most familiar passage in all the Bible, which expresses the heart and soul of scripture, is John 3:16,17: "For God so loved the *world* that He gave His only begotten Son, that *whoever* believes in Him should not perish but have everlasting life. For

God did not send His Son into the world to condemn the world, but that the *world* through Him might be saved." In these two verses "the world" is used four times, and this repetition reveals how broad is our Father's heart concern.

Those words in John chapter 3 were originally spoken by the Lord Jesus to one of the Jewish leaders, Nicodemus. They spelled out a concept that was entirely new to him. He and his fellow Israelites were convinced that they, the seed of Abraham, were God's chosen people and the Gentiles were merely unworthy outcasts. In fact no one but a Jew was even allowed to enter God's temple. So they just couldn't imagine God *loving the whole world.*

We see, however, that John the Baptist had already brought this truth into bold focus when he introduced the Lord Jesus to the Jews at the Jordan River. He called out, "Behold! The Lamb of God who takes away the sin of the *world!*" (Jn. 1:29)

It was Paul who gave the strongest appeal to his fellow Hebrew countrymen. He put it very straight when he asked them, "Is He the God of the Jews only? Is He not *also* the God of the Gentiles? *Yes*, of the Gentiles also." (Rom. 3:29)

In essence, we readily agree that "He is also the God of the Gentiles", for we ourselves are Gentiles. But often without realizing it, we are as closed to the spiritual needs of the many *unreached people groups* of our world today as Nicodemus was. Recently I looked over a list of churches in Orange County, California, where we now live. I found listed over a thousand in this one county alone! And a number of these are "mega-churches" with congregations in the thousands. In addition, we have scores of Christian ministries working with special groups (street people, prisoners, etc.), plus dozens of Christian radio and TV broadcasts.

Right next door is the much more populous Los Angeles County. In that area there are several times more churches and Christian outreaches. Think then, of how many Christian groups and ministries we have throughout the whole of our nation.

The Lord Jesus surely intended to divert some of this attention away from ourselves when He gave His discourse on the "Good Shepherd". He declared, "*Other sheep* I have which are not of this fold; them *also* I *must bring*, and they will hear My voice; and there will be one flock and one shepherd." (Jn. 10:16)

We find the same emphasis again in II Cor. 5:19: "God was in Christ, reconciling the *world* to Himself." And the Apostle John echoes the same in his epistles. "He Himself is the propitiation for our sins, and *not for ours only* but also for the *whole world.*" (I Jn. 4:14)

The natural conclusion of all this comes from Paul's plea in Romans 10:14,15: "How then shall they [the other half of the world] believe in Him of whom they have not heard? And how shall they hear without a preacher? And how shall they preach unless they are *sent?*" Yes, those who have received the gospel are to *send* messengers to those who have not heard. But we Christians in America must overcome our seeming inertia toward this charge we've been given!

A Look at the "Ends of the Earth"

Now let us stand on the other side, and view things as they are today in much of the "third world". I have in my hand a monthly publication called the "Global Prayer Digest". This little magazine is put out by the U.S. Center for World Missions in Pasadena, California. Each issue highlights the need of the unreached people groups in a given country. On some months they show several scattered groups with similar religious backgrounds.

A few months ago the country in focus was Nigeria. This moderate sized nation in the heart of Africa has eighty unreached people groups. Just to give you an idea of their needs, I will quote a few lines about these neglected tribes:

On Day 8 in this Prayer Digest we were introduced to the Gurdu people and then told that "*none* of the Gurdus know about Jesus."

On Day 14 we learned about the background of the Manga people, and were informed that "Not one of the 200,000 Mangas is a Christian."

On Day 17 they told us about the Kanuri people, then mentioned that "there are less than 20 known Christians among the 3,500,000 Kanuris."

On Day 23 they explained a good bit about the Housa people, and stated that "the 20,600,000 Housas are 99.9% Muslim."

On Day 29 we were exposed to the ways of the Abewa people, then it was reported that "not one Abewa has accepted Christ."

Note – there are *eighty* of these unreached people groups in Nigeria alone. And throughout the rest of Africa, Asia, the Middle East and former Russia there are *hundreds and hundreds* of similar situations!

Our Father in heaven looks down on their blindness and bondage, and urges us His people to "pray the Lord of the harvest to send out laborers into His harvest." (Lk. 10:2)

Here I must share something which recently took place in one of the villages in Taiwan where the Village Gospel Mission is working. A lady had accepted the Lord and been baptized in the little church. But then her idolatrous husband and relatives forbade her to go to any meetings. So one Sunday morning she sent her young daughter to deliver a small package to the pastor. When he opened it he found a single rose with a brief note attached. It read, "I'm so sorry I won't be able to come to services anymore, for my family will not allow it. But from the bottom of my heart I want to thank you for caring enough to come to this out of the way place to tell us about Jesus."

I imagine that this little message caused the angels in heaven to shed tears of joy. And I know that surely our Father's heart was very pleased.

Conversing with our Father

When you communicate with your Father, what do you talk to Him about? There was a time when the Lord's disciples asked Him to teach them to pray. He began in a very straight-forward manner. "When you pray, this is what you are to say: *'Our Father in heaven, ...'"*

The question arises, why did He specify "Our Father *in heaven*"? This immediately helps us to position our asking from His point of view, to look at things as Heaven sees them, to adjust our concerns as fitting for the children of God.

The Lord Jesus' perspective on all that He did was in perfect alignment with His Father's desires. On one occasion He said, "*My food* is to do the will of Him who sent me, and to *finish His work.* Do you not say, 'There are still four months and then comes the harvest? Behold, I say to you, *lift up your eyes* and *look at the fields,* for they are already white for harvest!" (Jn. 4:34,35)

The Lord's meat and drink was to see His Father's will accomplished. He called it "finishing His work." Then He at once tied it to the unreaped harvest. It has now been 2,000 years since the Lord spoke those words, and His Father's work has still not been finished. In fact, in much of the world it has not yet even begun. Many fields are still waiting to be harvested.

The next thing He taught His disciples to pray was **"Hallowed be Your name."** In English, these four words are too condensed to give the full intended meaning. The original Greek reads, "Let your name be reverenced as holy." And in other languages, such as the Chinese translation, the full connotation is: "May *all men everywhere* honor your name as holy – as the highest name above all names."

Yes, after aligning our perspectives with our Father in heaven, we then begin to pray that all over the world *His name* will be worshipped and adored. In far too many regions of the world today, it is sad to see *other names* being exalted. One billion Muslims consider the loveless, inflexible, fatalistic Allah to be the highest name. Another billion Buddhists esteem the names of their fearsome and often cruel gods. Still thousands of other strange gods are worshipped among 800 million Hindus. And 200 million atheists revere no name for God at all. Why is the name of our Father, the true and living God, not honored among them? Because the bulk of them know nothing about Him.

Now our prayers are to move on to the request: *"May Your kingdom come."* This is not just a plea for the day when the Lord Jesus will return to earth and set up His physical kingdom. Our Father desires His kingdom to move in *now* and be established in areas where Satan's kingdom has been flourishing.

In fact, the Lord Jesus' first set of parables – His *kingdom parables* – were meant to encourage the planting of His kingdom. The first tells of *the sower who went out to sow.* The second states that *the field is the world.* The third describes the phenomenal *growth* of the tiny mustard seed which becomes a great tree with spreading branches. Then comes the story of the yeast [the gospel] mixed into three huge batches of flour [the whole world] until it *all* was leavened. Next is the account of the man who bought a *whole field* because there was treasure hidden in it. Then came the merchant who was *in search of beautiful pearls.* And last is the story of the *net cast into the sea*, which caught fish of all kinds. All these parables shed light for us as we pray "May Your kingdom come."

Then the Lord taught us to pray, *"Your will be done on earth as it is in heaven."* This should surely lead us to ask, "How would You want me and my church to fit into Your world plan?" For to truly seek *"His will"* means following His *heartbeat.*

Before we close this chapter, I feel we must share a few more pictures of our Father's heart from the book He has given us. The first appears in the final verse of the book of Jonah. The Lord asks that reluctant missionary prophet a moving question: "Should I not pity Nineveh, that great city in which are more than 120,000 persons who [spiritually] cannot discern between their right hand and their left?"

Much later, when Jesus was on earth, we observe an attitude which was quite the opposite of Jonah's: "When He [the Lord Jesus] saw the multitudes, He was moved with *compassion* for them, because they were weary and scattered like sheep having no shepherd. Then He said to His disciples, 'The harvest truly is plentiful, but the laborers are few. Therefore *pray* the Lord of the harvest *to send out laborers* into His harvest.'" (Matt. 9:36-38) He longs for His compassion for the multitudes of those without a shepherd to become the driving force of our prayer life.

Then going back to that first Christmas evening when the angel appeared to the shepherds with a breathtaking announcement, we hear him declare: "Behold, I bring you good tidings of great joy which shall be *to all people*." (Lk. 2:10)

And regarding prayer, we see the Lord's heart concern when He cleansed the temple in Jerusalem. In the midst of His outbreak of intense emotion, He quoted from the prophet Isaiah: "My house shall be called a house of prayer *for all nations*."

Certainly it is in our missionary outreach to the overlooked people groups, and our earnest prayers for them, that we most closely share our Father's heartbeat.

CHAPTER 5

Jesus Passes
the Baton

In our last chapter we looked at world missions as viewed from the heart of our Father. Now we want to hear the Lord Jesus' thoughts, since He was the leading missionary of all history. He was *"sent"* into the world by His Father; He mentions this fifty times. To "send" and to "be sent" are missionary terms. And you can't have one without the other. Missionaries today must have those who send them. In fact, every one who goes needs a good number of committed senders to stand behind him, bearing him up in many ways. More of this later, but let us note that our Father desires *all* His children to be involved in reaching the world with the good news of salvation, either by sending or being sent.

In this chapter we will look at how the Lord Jesus sent forth His twelve disciples as missionaries, and how He insured that His program of world missions would continue until His return. In a real sense, the missionary enterprise is like a relay race. After each lap, the baton must be carefully and decisively passed on to the next generation. Actually one reason so many of

the world's people groups are without the gospel today is that the baton was not securely passed on.

The Lord Jesus surely did His part, handing the baton to the next generation, and He desires each missionary, pastor, youth worker and parent to do the
same. In chapter one I told the story of how the baton
was passed on to me. Now we want to see how the
Lord sought to transmit the primary burden of His heart.
It was He who ran the first lap. He set the pace. And
now He says to each of us, "Follow Me."

"It Is Finished"

"It is finished" was the last sentence the Lord Jesus
uttered when He hung there on the cross. God's great
plan of redemption had been completed. The Savior's
sacrifice of Himself for man's sin was *finished*. So He
committed His spirit to God. His body was buried, and
after three days He arose from the tomb. Then what
happened? Rather, what did not happen? Surprisingly,
He *did not* immediately return to heaven.

Instead, He remained here on earth for forty more
days. Why? For two reasons, which are spelled out in
Acts 1:3. "He presented Himself *alive* after His suffering by many infallible *proofs*, being seen by them [His
disciples] during forty days and *speaking* of the things
pertaining to the *kingdom of God*." First, He used those
days to amply establish the evidence for His being alive
after His resurrection. Secondly, as we shall see, it
was no simple job to pass on the baton of missions.
That required sustained and repeated effort.

He had paid the price for the sins of the world. But
unless the people of the world are informed of this provision, all is lost! It would be the tragedy of all trag-
edies! So, over a period of forty days, He used every

means to engrave this charge on the hearts of His disciples. The placing of this responsibility squarely on the shoulders of His followers, we call His "Great Commission."

Jesus had spoken about "the kingdom of God" many times during His three years of ministry, but now It was different. He, the King of God's kingdom, was ready to plant the beginnings of His rule throughout the world. Missions must be done on a world-wide scale. This is the way the Father and Son look at it, and would have us look at it.

One reason for the urgency in presenting His commission was the passive attitude of His disciples. The Holy Spirit had not yet come with His empowering, and their fleshly minds just couldn't seem to grasp the significance of what He was trying to get across. In fact, at the end of the forty days, just minutes before He was taken up from them, they asked, "Lord, will You at this time *restore the kingdom to Israel?*" (Acts 1:6) They were still focused on their own narrow, self-centered desires. This must have grieved Him, as a passive attitude toward missions always does.

Now, let us examine the various presentations of His Great Commission. There were probably a good many occasions during those forty days when He discussed this longing of His heart with them, but there are five occurrences recorded in scripture. In each of these, His presentation is different. We can see Him phrasing it in every possible way.

A Partnership

The first record of the Lord Jesus delivering the Great Commission to His disciples is right after His resurrection, at the end of the Gospel of Matthew. "And

Jesus came and spoke to them saying, 'All authority has been given to Me in heaven and on earth. Go therefore and make disciples of all nations, baptizing them in the name of the Father and of the Son and of the Holy Spirit, teaching them to observe all things that I have commanded you; and lo, I am with you always, even to the end of the age.'"

There are several particulars within these verses which we need to note. First of all is the partnership which the Lord set up between Himself and His disciples. For the previous three years He had been with them in a rather simple, straight-forward relationship. He was their "teacher", their "Rabbi", their leader who made all the decisions and filled in all the details. All they needed to do was listen and follow along.

But from now on it would be different. On that last night in the "upper room", He repeatedly informed them that He soon would be leaving them. Yet He would still be with them, in quite a new manner. Physically they would "see Him no more", and yet He promised, "Lo, I am with you always, even to the end of the age." Now His presence would carry a new degree of power. "All authority has been given to Me in heaven and on earth." He would be sitting at the right hand of God, still ready to direct all their operations, but from now on it would be they who did the going and the making of disciples.

He had said before, "I will build My church, and the gates of Hades shall not prevail against it." (Mt. 16:18) But they (and we) were to learn that He accomplishes the building of His church by means of a partnership. He sends His messengers backed up by all His authority. They go, with trust and confidence.

There have been certain periods during the past 2,000 years when this partnership has worked out well.

But sad to say, there have also been periods when it has floundered. Why? Certainly He was always there to do His part. But now we will begin to see one cause for that failure as we look at the next part of His commission.

"Make disciples of all nations ... teaching them to observe *all things* that I have commanded you." Unfortunately, there frequently came breakdowns in the teaching of *all the things* He had taught them. There was inadequate passing on of the Great Commission from one generation to the next. Their "disciples" did not always function as such. Many churches became ingrown and let the rest of the world go by. So the forward advance slowed down, and the enemy's false religions gained ground.

When God's people lose sight of "all the nations", His Great Commission is neglected. The world enters a partial eclipse which is painful and unfair to those who live in darkness.

"All the World ... to every Creature"

The next account of commissioning His disciples is at the end of Mark's gospel. "And He said to them, 'Go into *all the world* and preach the gospel to *every creature* [person]. He who believes and is baptized will be saved; but he who does not believe will be condemned.'" He made it absolutely clear that every person in all the world is to have the opportunity to hear and understand His gospel. That does not mean that they will all believe. No, most will not, for previously the Lord had said, "The gate is small and the way is narrow that leads to life, and there are few who find it." (Mt. 7:13 NIV)

When we begin to think about His charge here in Mark, that *every person in the world* should have a fair chance to comprehend the salvation message, we see at once that a lot of "going" and "sending" is required. Today there are over five billion people in the world, and probably half of these have not yet truly heard.

This sad circumstance brings us face to face with a related problem. What about those two or three billion who have not heard? How can they be doomed when they have never heard? Some feel that since "God is love", He surely wouldn't punish those who never knew of Christ's redemption. On the other hand, some feel that all who do not believe in Jesus Christ, even those who have not heard, are slated for intense, eternal suffering.

After much study and thought, I believe the truth lies somewhere between these two poles. True, our God is filled with love, and yet He has a hatred for sin. We must remember His other qualities as well. He is absolutely *just*, and He is infinitely *wise*.

God's word refers over eight hundred times to being "righteous" or "upright". And there are over one hundred references to "justice" or being "just". Some of these apply directly to God's final judgments, and we will quote just a few.

"He shall *judge* the world in *righteousness*, and He shall administer *judgment* for the peoples in *righteousness*." *(Ps. 9:8)*

"*Righteousness and justice* are the foundation of *His throne*." (Ps. 97:2)

"With *righteousness* He shall *judge* the world, and the people with *equity*." (Ps. 98:9)

"O Lord of hosts, You who *judge righteously*, testing the mind and the heart." (Jer. 11:20)

These verses imply that there will be *degrees* of
punishment, depending on the many factors involved
in every person's life. This is again borne out in some
of the more specific references regarding the final judgment days. The Lord Jesus, for instance, in speaking
to those who utterly refused to accept Him or His disciples, declared that it would be *"more tolerable"* for
the wicked city of Sodom in the day of judgment, than
for such people. (Lk. 10:12)

Also, in regard to that last end-time judgment, as it
is described at the close of the book of Revelation, it
states: "they were judged each one *according to his
works."* (Rev. 20:13)

Then when we give thought to the *wisdom* of God,
and look at the various aspects of His creation, we
become overwhelmed at His understanding. The closer
we examine both the infinitesimally small and the in-
comprehensibly large, we are astounded beyond measure at His omniscience. The particles and sub-par-
ticles that form the nucleus of the atom, the phenomenal complexity of the billions of cells that make up all
the functioning parts of each human body, along with
the far reaches of the hundred billion galaxies, are all
controlled by predictable laws and precise forces. *Certainly He is too wise to do anything unwise.*

All these reasonings, however, bear two sides.
Another consideration is that God's judgments will involve us believers as well as the unbelievers. We know
well that those of us who believe in the Lord Jesus and
have accepted Him as our Lord, will be able to enjoy
the beauties and blessings of heaven forever. But for

each of us the scale of *rewards* will vary. The extent of our "*treasures* in heaven" will depend on the quality of our lives and *our labors* for Him. "The Son of Man will come in the glory of His Father with His angels, and then He will *reward each according to his works.*" (Mt. 16:27) And surely one relevant factor will be the extent to which we have involved ourselves in His program to reach the whole world with His gospel, so that each person has a chance to hear.

Comprehending the Scriptures

The third account of the commissioning of His disciples is found in the last chapter of the Gospel of Luke. "He opened their understanding, that they might *comprehend the scriptures.* Then He said to them, 'Thus *it is written*, and thus it was necessary for the Christ to suffer and to rise from the dead the third day, and that repentance and remission of sins should be preached in His name *to all nations*, beginning at Jerusalem. And you are witnesses of these things." (Lk. 24:45-48)

A very significant point to note here is that this third presentation was prefaced by a very special action. The Lord *opened their understanding* so that they could begin to get a better grasp of the essential message of the scriptures. He had of course been teaching them God's Word for three years. But several times they just seemed unspeakably dense. And we find Him on occasion having to ask them, "Do you not yet perceive nor understand? Is your heart still hardened? Having eyes, do you not see, and having ears, do you not hear?" (Mk. 8:17,18) And even after His resurrection He had to scold them for being "slow of heart." Then as He finally sought to lay on them His mission to reach the world with the gospel, they seemed totally unable to grasp it. So it is not surprising that He reached the point where He needed to "open their understanding that they might comprehend the scriptures."

Even so, they didn't "wake up" immediately. It took time, quite a bit of time. They did get a helpful boost, however, with the coming of the Holy Spirit. For a few days before, on the night preceding His crucifixion, as He introduced to them the soon coming arrival of the Spirit, He specifically pointed to a much needed phase of the Spirit's work. "The Helper, the Holy Spirit, whom the Father will send in My name, will *teach* you all things, and *bring to your remembrance* all things that I said to you." (Jn. 14:26) And then a few minutes later He went over it again. "I still have many things to say to you, but you cannot bear them now. However, when He, the Spirit of truth, has come, *He will guide you into all truth.*" (Jn. 16:12)

What a strengthening came from those two aids! First, that He opened their understanding, then eventually gave them their special Teacher, the Holy Spirit. It makes a great difference in our own lives if we periodically ask Him to open our understanding and teach us by the Spirit.

Another point of real consequence is that immediately after He opened their understanding, He said to them "*It is written,*" and He proceeded to sum up the three main pillars of scripture. First was that *Christ must suffer,* second was that He would *rise from the dead,* and third that the remission of sins should be *preached to all nations.* His simple synopsis of scripture was composed of *these three* core truths: His cross, His resurrection, and His commission.

If someone were to ask you what was the main message of scripture, how would you answer? We would probably all reply that the heart of God's Word is the cross. Some might go a step further and mention the cross and the resurrection. But rarely do we hear people mention all three.

I accepted the Lord when I was eight years old. Now I am seventy-eight. And you can be sure that during these past seventy years I have heard a lot of sermons, joined in the singing of many hymns and gospel songs, and listened to numerous fellow Christians share their testimonies. These have been a great blessing to me, and I am a fortunate person indeed to have been allowed such a mountain of treasures. But as I look back on it all, one thing does concern me, and that is the lack of emphasis given to the *"third pillar," which is His Great Commission.*

Recently I received a catalogue of Christian books. It offered a general spread of all conceivable kinds of evangelical books, commentaries, Bibles, etc. Well over two thousand items were included. Yet I couldn't find one book on world missions mentioned in their listings.

A similar situation seems to exist in many Christian bookstores. I called a a large one near us recently to ask about titles regarding world missions. The clerk wasn't sure at first whether they had any, but finally found one on the computer which they would have to order if I requested it. Such circumstances are a somber index of the mentality of many Christians today toward our Lord's Great Commission. Therefore, it is not surprising that so many people groups throughout the world are still living in darkness.

Peace to You

The fourth account of giving His charge to the disciples comes near the end of the Gospel of John. "Jesus came and stood in the midst, and said to them 'Peace be with you.' When He had said this, He showed them His hands and His side. Then the disciples were glad when they saw the Lord. So Jesus said to them *again*, 'Peace be to you! As the Father has sent Me, I also send you.' And when He had said this, *He breathed on them* and said to them, 'Receive the Holy Spirit'." (Jn. 20:19-22)

On this occasion the Lord especially shared with them an element of comfort. Twice He poured forth that soothing balm of His "peace" because He knew how much they would need it. Showing them His hands and His side actually was to hold a double meaning for them. At the time however, it evoked but one thought in their minds. Those wound marks in His hands and His side proved conclusively that He was indeed their resurrected Master. And this of course comforted them immensely. In fact the text says, "They were *glad* when they saw the Lord."

His next statement, however, would eventually bring about quite a different consideration. "*As* the Father has sent Me, I also send you." That little word "as" in the original Greek text carries the meaning "in the same manner." So a reflection on this statement brings other thoughts to mind.

For one, it implies that since His being sent by the Father produced the wounds and scars which He had just shown them, His sending them might very well produce some wounds and scars too. But the compensation for that possibility was again His supernatural "*peace.*"

Another consideration is that *just as* the Father in sending Him meant the continual enabling of the Holy Spirit, *so they* could count on the same enablement. In fact, His very next encouragement to them, right at that moment, was to "receive the Holy Spirit."

The rather strange action of "breathing on them" also had meaningful significance. It was as if He were breathing out His innermost life (with all of its love, power, wisdom and the fruits of the Spirit) to be breathed in by them. *As* the Father had anointed Him with the Spirit, so was He anointing them.

Then there is one more word in this passage which calls for our attention. It is that word "sent" or "send", which He used twice. We frequently hear young people ask, "What constitutes a missionary call?" Or "How do I know if the Lord wants me to go as a missionary?" These are valid questions and worthy of careful attention. When one of the Lord's disciples begins to feel an urging in his spirit to venture forth to some unreached area, how reassuring it is if at the same time, a group of God's people feel called to *send* him.

The Lord does His sending through His churches. That is why He is so pleased when a church becomes serious and zealous about supporting His messengers to reach those people groups which as yet have no church. He is delighted whenever He sees a congregation educating its people to become involved in His sending program. It has been said that to properly care for one person who is sent, there need to be about a hundred senders. So if you are not one of those being sent, He wants to involve you as a sender.

The Ends of the Earth

The final meeting with His disciples came at the end of that forty day period, just before He departed back to heaven. Once again He laid before them His Great Commission: "'You shall receive power when the Holy Spirit has come upon you; and you shall be witnesses to Me in Jerusalem, and in all Judea and Samaria, and *to the ends of the earth.*' Now when He had spoken these things, while they watched He was taken up, and a cloud received Him out of their sight." (Acts 1:8,9)

It should truly move us to realize that our Savior's last six words as He left this planet were, "to the ends of the earth." The first part of His command was for them to be His witnesses in Jerusalem, then Judea and Samaria. Our "Jerusalem" (our own home location) is of course our first responsibility. But Jerusalem is to be only the first step. It is regrettable when Jerusalem is all we see and work for. In fact the next few chapters of the book of Acts show the Lord's disappointment with that early church for getting bogged down in Jerusalem. He had to allow severe persecution to come on that city and "they were all scattered." A few years later the city was actually destroyed. Also, throughout the remainder of the book of Acts little is said even about Judea and Samaria. The emphasis is on "the ends of the earth."

Surely our Lord is immensely concerned about the unreached extremities, those regions which still do not know of His salvation. He laid down His life for them, and purchased their redemption at infinite cost. And He gave the last forty days of His time here on earth to commissioning His disciples and urging them to pass on the baton. How He must long for each one of us to share this burden and concern.

What if the Christians of every church in America today took to heart our Lord's Great Commission? Like a prudent investment company, what if they poured over plans and maps and charts, holding consultations to see how to apply all their assets toward reaching the ends of the earth? Surely it wouldn't take long to cover the globe with the gospel.

We thank God for the churches where this sort of thing is going on, and you can be sure those churches are experiencing blessing from the Lord. In this computer age, it is conceivable that world missions could soon be shifted into high gear. In closing, let us look again at our Lord's powerful statement:

"I am the Light of the world. He who follows Me [having learned about Me] shall not walk in darkness, but shall have the light of life." (Jn. 8:12) What a joy to see pitiable pagan people who have been living in darkness, delivered over into the "light of life"!

CHAPTER 6

The Role of the Spirit

It is evident that each member of the Trinity is greatly concerned for world missions. We have already looked at the passion burning in the heart of the Father and the Son. Now it is time to examine the missionary role of the Spirit.

We could well call Him the "Director of Operations" or the "Power Supply" for the missionary enterprise. His arrival ten days after the Lord ascended was actually what launched the take-off of missions.

The Lord Jesus had twice directed His disciples to wait for the Spirit's coming before they began their missionary undertakings. "Behold I send the promise of My Father upon you; but tarry in the city of Jerusalem until you are endued with power from on high." (Lk. 24:49) "And being assembled together with them, He commanded them not to depart from Jerusalem, but to wait for the Promise of the Father... "You shall be baptized with the Holy Spirit not many days from now." (Acts 1:4,5)

Surely the Lord Jesus would have us become aware of a basic spiritual law regarding missions. *Every part* of the missionary enterprise – from educating God's people to the sending, going, empowering, harvesting and discipling – all must be done by His Spirit. The prophet Zechariah's words surely apply here. "'Not by [human] might nor by [human] power, but by My Spirit,' says the Lord of Hosts."

The Spirit of Missions

Now let us take a look at the account of the Spirit's coming. "When the Day of Pentecost was fully come, they were all with one accord in one place. And suddenly there came a sound from heaven, as of *a rushing, mighty wind*, and it filled the whole house where they were sitting. Then there appeared to them divided tongues, as of *fire*, and one sat upon each of them. And they were filled with the Holy Spirit and began to speak with other [foreign] tongues, as the Spirit gave them utterance. And there were dwelling in Jerusalem Jews, devout men, *from every nation under heaven*. And when this sound occurred, the multitude came together, and were confused, because everyone heard them speak in his own language. Then they were amazed and marveled, saying to one another,

'Look, are not all these who speak Galileans? And how is it that *we hear each in our own language in which we were born?* ...We hear them speaking in our own tongues the wonderful works of God.'" *(Acts 2:1-11)*

Here it is! A mighty, supernatural *missionary* event taking place right there in Jerusalem, as soon as the Holy Spirit arrived. He came as a mighty rushing wind. He lit the disciples afire and through them began to speak forth "the wonderful works of God" to men "from every nation under heaven," and to each in his own language.

It all fitted in perfectly with the Lord's final words just as He was leaving earth. "You shall receive *power* when the *Holy Spirit* has come upon you; and you shall be witnesses to Me in Jerusalem, and in all Judea and Samaria, and to the ends of the earth." What a massive demonstration of world missions took place within just a few minutes of the Holy Spirit's arrival. Without delay He exhibited His power and involvement in God's missionary program.

Perhaps before we proceed further, we should give some thought as to what is meant by *"power."* This is a term used a great deal by scientists and engineers. According to definition "power is a measure of the amount of work done per unit of time." Or we might say that power is shown by the accomplishment attained in an hour or a day or a year. Now as we look at all the Holy Spirit achieved for world missions in one hour or less, we have a tremendous display of *power.* "Men from every nation under heaven" heard "the wonderful works of God," each in his own mother tongue! And this is the kind of power our Lord is primarily interested in.

I remember attending a conference where about sixty missionaries were gathered for several days to discuss which techniques or strategies could be employed to bring about more results in our work. Finally at the end of our prolonged deliberations, one brother stood up and gave this testimony. He said, "I have found that when the Holy Spirit is working, most any method works. But when the Holy Spirit is not working, nothing seems to work." He sat down, and as far as I was concerned, the conference was over!

There is a place, of course, for Christian leaders to get together and share their experiences and insights.

Wise old Solomon three times in the book of Proverbs
made such statements as "In the multitude of counselors there is safety." (Prov. 11:14) But we must always
remember that man's counsel is still very much sec-
ondary to the enablement of the Holy Spirit. This is
what we want to substantiate in this chapter.

The Personnel Director

Now let us look at how the Holy Spirit selected two
of His choice missionaries, Barnabas and Paul, and sent
them out from the church at Antioch. "As they *minis-
tered to the Lord and fasted,* the Holy Spirit said, 'Now
separate to Me Barnabas and Saul [Paul] for the work
to which I have called them.' Then, having *fasted and
prayed,* and laid hands on them, they sent them away.
So, *being sent out by the Holy Spirit,* they went..." (Acts
13:2-4)

Here we are looking at a very spiritual church and
one involved in missions. Here is a church that "min-
istered to the Lord and fasted." The Holy Spirit became very involved in their activities. And as He became involved, He began to send out missionaries.

One of the initial requirements for world missions
to expand is that individuals be "called", or "sent." How
does this come about? The Lord Jesus clearly dealt
with this issue and gave us distinct instructions on how
to see it accomplished. "Then He said to them, 'The
harvest truly is great, but the laborers are few; therefore *pray the Lord of the harvest* to send out laborers
into His harvest.'" (Lk. 10:2)

From the account of what happened in the church at
Antioch and a few other references, it appears that the
Holy Spirit is to be viewed as "the Lord of the harvest."
First, He is or should be the prime-mover in the sending.

Let us look at how Luke opens his introduction to the book of Acts. "The former account [the Gospel of Luke] I made, O Theophilus, of all that Jesus began both to do and teach, until the day in which He was taken up, after He *through the Spirit* had given commandments to the apostles whom He had chosen." (Acts 1:1,2) Here at the very start, it is the Lord sending out His first missionaries *"through the Spirit."*

This means that when a church is being led and carried along by the Holy Spirit, its members are in a position to ask the "Lord of the harvest" to send out missionaries. He is really very eager to do this. In fact He is longing to do it. But sometimes He has to wait until we are also eager and longing for Him to do it. What indications might He be looking for? Two elements which are mentioned twice regarding the church of Antioch are *prayer* and *fasting*.

I wonder what experience you have had in fasting along with your praying? I know of a good number of Christians who have seen very encouraging results as they have involved themselves in this spiritual exercise. It seems to be a means of drawing us especially near to the Lord. The scriptures invite us to 'Draw near to God and He will draw near to you." (Jas. 4:8) The Lord held out a similar motivation to His people through Jeremiah His prophet: "I know the thoughts that I think toward you, says the Lord, thoughts of peace and not of evil, to give you a future and a hope. Then you will call upon Me and go and pray to Me, and I will listen to you. And you will seek Me and find Me *when you search for Me with all your heart."* (Jer. 29:11-13)

Fasting can often help us to seek Him with all our heart. There are about seventy references to fasting in the scriptures, and they make it clear that God truly honors such extra devotion by His people. His Spirit at such times often moves in uplifting and encouraging ways.

We might get started in fasting by just foregoing one meal a month. Some of us as we get older, or others because of poor health, may find even one meal difficult to give up. Such was the case with the prophet Daniel in his later years. When he was nearly ninety he could handle only a partial fast. So he left off fancy foods and lived on simple fare for a period of three weeks. This was pleasing to the Lord, and as a result he was granted exceptional insight into God's working.

L.E. Maxwell, founder of Prairie Bible Institute in Alberta, Canada, was used of the Lord to train many young people for the mission field. A helpful piece of advice which he gave to each one before they went out was, "When you feel spiritually weak, give yourself to fasting and prayer. When the enemy is attacking you, give yourself to fasting and prayer. When you are short of funds, give yourself to fasting and prayer. When you are discouraged, give yourself to fasting and prayer."

I have come to know a number of those Prairie Bible Institute missionaries and find them to be workers whom the Holy Spirit is really using. That church at Antioch was certainly on the right track. Their missionaries were "sent out by the Holy Spirit." And you can be sure they were sustained by the Spirit because of the prayer support of their church back in Antioch.

The Strategist

Paul was gifted when it came to thinking through missionary strategy. He usually had good understanding of conditions even in those areas which he had not

yet reached. But his own abilities to plan effective
missionary strategy were a far cry from the wisdom of
the Holy Spirit. We all do well to ask the Holy Spirit to
be the one to open and close doors for us. He is the
supreme, all-wise strategist.

Let us focus on one incident in the missionary trav
els of Paul and his party. "When they had gone through
Phrygia and the region of Galatia, they were forbidden
by the Holy Spirit to preach the word in Asia [Asia Mi-
nor]. After they had come to Mysia, they tried to go
into Bethynia, but the Spirit did not permit them. So
passing by Mysia, they came down to Troas. And a
vision appeared to Paul in the night. A man of
Macedonia stood and pleaded with him saying, 'Come
over to Macedonia and help us.' Now after he had
seen the vision, immediately we sought to go to
Macedonia, *concluding* that the Lord had called us to
preach the gospel to them.' (Acts 16:6-10)

There are several things we can learn from this
passage. The first is that Paul, with all his brilliance,
was wrong twice in his evaluation of where he and his
team should go. When he looked at Asia Minor, he
saw it as a very needy, unreached area deserving of
the gospel, so he decided to proceed in that direction.
But the Holy Spirit saw things that Paul and his team
members didn't see. Paul's next decision was to move
up into Bythinea, another needy place. But again the
Holy Spirit did not consider this to be the wisest venture.

What does the Holy Spirit see that we don't? He
can see what is going on inside men's hearts. Or, to
state it another way, He knows when a person or district is ripe and ready for the gospel. If a certain region
has no hunger for spiritual truth, it could be a great

waste of time and effort to start laboring there at that time. But later on things might be very different.

However, when our plans are stopped, that doesn't mean we just quit. Paul's plans were stopped twice, but he still moved ahead. He didn't turn around and go home. He had the heart of a missionary, and he had the Lord's Great Commission ringing in his ears. In fact years later when Peter began his first epistle, he mentioned the Christians in Bithynia as one of the groups he was writing to. So when the Holy Spirit forbade Paul to go into Bithynia, He had other plans to reach those people. Therefore we see that it is just as significant for the Holy Spirit to close a door as to open one. If the door to an unripe field were not closed, we would probably not proceed to the riper harvest. So we ought not be discouraged when some of our plans are halted.

I remember a situation in the province of Szechwan in western China, when the Communists were drawing near to occupy that area. The people became extremely fearful, and began to flock to the meetings in the churches. It was at that time that the Holy Spirit seemed to lead many of His people to that area to conduct special evangelistic meetings. People came out to these meetings in unusual numbers, and many turned to the Lord. The time was ripe for a harvest. Even though the Lord was closing the door as far as the missionaries were concerned (they had to leave), the Holy Spirit was opening the door to many hearts. The Lord reminded Isaiah that His ways are not always the same as our ways, but His ways are higher and better than our ways. (Is. 55:8,9) When the Lord closed the door to all missionaries in China, the Holy Spirit still led fifty million Chinese into new life.

Another lesson we can learn from Paul's experience is that the Lord speaks to us to communicate His will in different ways. We are not given the details of how the Holy Spirit hindered Paul and his team from entering both Asia Minor and Bythinia, but we are told they were directed to Macedonia by a "vision" in the night. Some feel that Paul had a *dream* where the man from Macedonia appeared to him and invited him to come.

Dreams as a rule are not valid means of obtaining guidance for our lives. But sometimes when these dreams are particularly vivid and seem to fit in perfectly with the circumstances, they are certainly worthy of consideration. It is also interesting to note how Paul and his team handled this "dream." It says, "After he had seen the vision, immediately we sought to go to Macedonia, *concluding* that the Lord had called us to preach the gospel to them." The wording of this sentence was according to Solomon's words: "In a multitude of counselors there is safety."

Had they been wrong in their deliberations, the Lord could easily have closed another door for them. He will surely do the same for us. Sometimes we feel people like Paul and other spiritual giants always had supernatural leading. But I have observed that usually the Lord's provision is Spirit-directed *wisdom*. One of my favorite and most used promises is James 1:5-7: "If *any of you* lacks *wisdom*, let him ask of God, who gives to all liberally and without reproach, and *it will be given* to him. But let him ask *in faith, with no doubting,* for he who doubts is like a wave of the sea driven and tossed by the wind. For let not that man suppose that he will receive anything from the Lord."

I do not find in God's Word any promise of direct *revelation*, but this promise of *wisdom* is so stated as to give us the greatest *assurance* possible. So we need never lack knowledge of at least the next step in the Holy Spirit's leading. Since He is our strategist, we don't want to *force* open any doors or go running ahead of Him. Wisdom means being wise, so the Holy Spirit wants to help us evaluate all the relevant factors and then come to a wise conclusion. If we still have no peace about our decision, this is a warning light, for *peace* is one of the fruits of the Spirit.

His Anointing

It would probably be safe to say that the greatest need of any missionary is to have the *anointing* of the Holy Spirit on his life and ministry. Most missionaries work with people who have grown up in a background of heathen beliefs. As a rule such people do not easily give up this ancestral heritage for a completely new and different "foreign religion." Therefore the missionary is often working against great odds from the start. How can he make his message *attractive* to opposing hearers?

The various words translated "anoint" or "anointing" in scripture are used over one hundred times. They refer to various occasions and purposes such as anointing kings or priests, the sick, or sacred furniture in the temple. But in nearly every case it consists of pouring on some fragrant, pleasing ointment. This is what the missionary needs to receive. He needs the Holy Spirit to anoint his personality and his message. He daily needs a fragrant, attractive approach as he introduces the gospel to people.

A prime example of this was when the Lord Jesus began His ministry. Luke quotes Isaiah's prophecy about Him: "The *Spirit of the Lord* is upon Me, because He has *anointed* Me to preach the gospel to the poor; He has sent me to heal the brokenhearted, to proclaim liberty to the captives and recovery of sight to the blind, to set at liberty those who are oppressed; to proclaim the acceptable year of the Lord." (Lk. 4:18,19)

What a fragrant, attractive approach! When the Spirit has anointed a missionary, there is a much better chance that people will be attracted to the true and living, loving God. Experienced missionary Paul, in the latter years of his ministry, said it this way: ""He who *establishes us with you* in Christ and has *anointed* us is God, who also has sealed us and *given us the Spirit* in our hearts as a guarantee." (II Cor. 1:21,22)

The Spirit's anointing does not mean that all will go smooth or easy, for this was not the case with either the Lord Jesus or the apostle Paul, and it is not usually so with today's effective missionaries. But in the end there will be far more accomplished if a missionary is *continually* being anointed by God's Spirit, than if he is just slugging away in his own strength.

We just spoke of being "continually" anointed, and this is precisely what is required. Just as perfume or other fragrance can fade, so can one's spiritual anointing. King David, who experienced forty years as Israel's monarch, had learned a lot about perfumes and fragrant aromas. And being the man of God he was, he could apply such truths to the spiritual realm. We find him writing these words: *"My strength* You have exalted like the wild ox, [for] I have been *anointed with fresh oil."* (Ps. 92:10)

There are times when we feel that we have sort of run down and need some time to get away and draw near to the Lord. An added incentive to do so can come from that chorus, "Spirit of the Living God, fall *afresh* on me."

The scriptures in many places reinforce this tactic as His approved means for spiritual restoration. "He gives power to the weak, and to those who have no might He increases strength. Even the youths shall faint and be weary, and the young men shall utterly fall. But those who *wait on the Lord* shall renew their strength; they shall mount up with wings like eagles; they shall run and not be weary; they shall walk and not faint." (Is. 40:29-31)

David, who wrote such beautiful Psalms, still had his down times, but he had learned how to recover his spirits and his strength. Over a dozen times we find him sharing his secret with us. Let us look at a couple of these.

"*Wait* on the Lord; be of good courage, and He shall strengthen your heart. *Wait,* I say, on the Lord.!" (Ps. 27:14)

"My soul, *wait* silently for God alone, for my expectation is from Him." (Ps. 62:5)

Jeremiah also discovered this wonderful remedy.

"The Lord is good to those who *wait* for Him, to the soul who seeks Him. It is good that one should hope and *wait* quietly for the salvation of the Lord. (Lam. 3:25,26)

Now, coming back to the Lord Jesus, let us look at how this principle operated in His life. "Then Jesus *returned* in the *power of the Spirit* to Galilee, and the news of Him went out through all the surrounding region. And He taught in their synagogues, *being glorified by all.*" (Lk. 4:14,15) He had just "returned" from a time alone out in the wilderness. We are told that He often retired to the desert, or up into the mountains to *wait on* His Father.

Every missionary greatly needs such "quiet" periods, for fresh anointings. But *we too* can set aside time alone, or in small groups together, to call upon the Lord in his behalf. As we have mentioned above, every missionary also needs a company of committed prayer partners to stand with him in the various aspects of his work. He truly needs *fresh anointings* if he is to maintain the power and fragrance of an effective ministry.

At the close of most of Paul's letters to his churches he, as a missionary, pled with them to help bear him up in prayer. He realized how much he continually needed fresh anointings on his life and ministry. Let us look at a couple of these.

"I beg you, brethren, through the Lord Jesus Christ, and *through the love of the Spirit*, that you strive together with me in prayers to God for me, that I may be delivered from those in Judea who do not believe, and that my service for Jerusalem may be acceptable." (Rom. 15:30,31)

Then to the Ephesian church he wrote:

"Praying always with all prayer and supplication *in the Spirit*, being watchful to this end with all perseverance and supplication for all the saints, and for me, *that utterance may be given to me*, that I...may speak boldly *as I ought to speak.*" (Eph. 6:18-20)

Related Parables

Two of the parables our Lord told apply particularly to the Holy Spirit and His involvement in missions. The first is in John 7: 38,39. "He who believes in Me, as the scripture has said, 'out of his heart will flow *rivers of living water.*' But this He spoke *concerning the Spirit.*" Rivers are channels which carry refreshing water for hundreds or thousands of miles. And the Lord says this is a picture of the Holy Spirit's work. It is also a picture of world missions.

The other parable was the last one He shared with His disciples on the night before He went to the cross. It began, "I am the *true vine*, and My Father is the vinedresser." Then a little further on He says, "He who *abides in Me, and I in him*, bears much fruit; for without Me you can do nothing." Then a little further on He adds, "You did not choose Me, but I chose you and *appointed you* that *you should go* and bear fruit, and that your fruit should remain." (Jn. l5: 1,5,16)

During this present age, the way Jesus abides in us is by His Spirit. So again, what He is saying is that apart from the Holy Spirit we can do nothing. Then He particularly applies this truth to missions when He says, "I chose you and appointed you *to go* and bear fruit."

Another reason we should see this as a missionary parable is that a *vine* is pictured. He doesn't refer here to a fig tree, an olive tree or other fruit trees which he spoke of on other occasions. In this final parable He draws our attention to the vine. If you are familiar with vines, you know that they consist of long branches reaching out much farther than branches of trees.

I remember a house I stayed in for a few days out on the east coast of Taiwan. It had a grape vine whose branches reached out to every part of the large front yard. I saw it as a beautiful metaphor for a missionary church. The Holy Spirit, the Spirit of missions, desires to grow fruit-bearing branches which will reach from your church around the world. And He longs to send forth rivers of living water which will flow to every corner of the earth.

CHAPTER 7

Pursuing God's Glory

So far in this book we have been looking at missions as they benefit people. Now it is time to insert a chapter from the other side. We have been pointing out how God loves people and desires them to know about the salvation which He provided at such great cost. But there is quite another approach to the whole issue of missions. **What does God benefit from it? Or what should God benefit from it?** It is only fitting that His glory should be proclaimed and known throughout all the earth.

Our God is worthy, worthy, worthy to be glorified. From the beginning of Genesis to the ending of Revelation, the scriptures exalt His glory. They lay down myriad considerations intended to show us how *qualified and deserving* He is to receive glory. Just to stimulate our thinking along this line, let us turn to some of these passages.

The Old Testament hymnbook, which is the Psalms, is not only filled with encouragements to praise the Lord, but David, the author of most of these beautiful poems, supports his doxologies by sound, solid justifications. Let's be reminded of just a few.

"The *heavens* declare the *glory* of God; and the firmament shows His handiwork." (Ps. 19:1) More and more astronomers, as they examine such data as the mass, energy, radiation and entropy of our universe, are seeing the hand of a glorious Creator. Now David was not an astrophysicist, and most of us are not. But like him we can say, "When I consider [give some serious thought to] Your heavens, the work of Your fingers, the moon and the stars which You have ordained, what is man that You are mindful of him?" (Ps. 8:3,4) Even a child can see greatness and magnificence as he looks up into the sky and then begins to ask questions.

David also takes a very deep breath when he looks around him and calls out, "O Lord, our Lord, how excellent is Your name in *all the earth.*" (Ps. 8:1) Chemists, physicists, geologists and biologists have been uncovering the wonders of our earth for generations now, and many of the marvels of their discoveries are so impressive they can only be properly acknowledged by awarding the highly esteemed Nobel prize. Yes, all the earth is filled with His glory.

Then another anthem comes from David's lips lauding a third aspect of God's grandeur. "I will praise You, for I am fearfully and wonderfully made. Marvelous are Your works, and that my soul knows very well." (Ps.139:14)

Each of the thousand trillion cells of our bodies is so complex and yet orderly in its construction, that even the experts are overwhelmed. Brilliant scientists have spent their lifetimes analyzing the various structures and mechanisms of the complicated and involved proteins, enzymes, hormones, DNA and RNA molecules which compose the essentials of every cell, and there is an increasing readiness to acknowledge "intelligent design."

Again, David was not a biochemist. But with even a modicum of reflection as we view the superb functions of our body parts we must conclude that truly these physiological wonders are exquisitely put together. So we too can only exclaim, "Marvelous are Your works, O Lord, and that my soul knows very well."

Now, to reinforce all this even further, let us skip over to the last book of the Bible and see how the majestic beings in the heavens view God's glory. "You are *worthy*, O Lord, to receive glory and honor and power, *for You created all things,* and by *Your will* they exist and were created." (Rev. 4:11) Yes, there is far too much systematic arrangement even in a blade of grass, for it all to have just *happened.* It is true that there are mutations and natural selection, but these can only operate where there is already life with its superbly functioning mechanisms.

Then in the next chapter of Revelation, the picture moves on to an even higher level of extolling His glory. *"Worthy is the Lamb who was slain* to receive power and riches and wisdom and strength and honor and glory and blessing!" (Rev. 5:12) Imagine the Creator of all things becoming a man and then giving Himself to be slain for all the gruesome sins of mankind which have accumulated since the beginning of history.

Finally, we must look at one more beautiful piece of homage sung by "a great multitude which no one could number, of all nations, tribes, peoples and tongues, standing before the throne and before the Lamb, clothed with white robes, with palm branches in their hands and crying with a loud voice saying, 'Salvation belongs to our God Who sits on the throne, and

to the Lamb!' All the angels stood around the throne
and the elders and the four living creatures and fell on
their faces before the throne and worshipped God saying, 'Amen, blessing and glory and wisdom, thanks-
giving and honor and power and might, be to our God
forever and ever. Amen.' ...And He Who sits on the
throne will dwell among them. They shall neither hunger any more nor thirst any more; the sun shall not
strike them, nor any heat, for the Lamb Who is in the
midst of the throne will shepherd them and lead them
to living fountains of waters. And God will wipe away
every tear from their eyes." (Rev. 7:9-12, 15-17) This
is a scene presenting the glory *due to God* because of
the *eternal blessings* which He has prepared for His redeemed children.

There are of course many other grounds given us
in scripture as to why God *should receive* unlimited
glory. If we allow ourselves to meditate on His
lovingkindness, His righteousness, justice, promises
and patience with us, our God surely *deserves* to be
glorified. And the unreached peoples of the world, who
live in spiritual darkness, have a right to know about
God's goodness, greatness and beautiful qualities so
that they too can come to know Him and give Him that
glory of which He is so worthy. This is what would
please Him to the utmost.

But (and here is one major reason why we so need
our missionary endeavors) during the bulk of human
history He has not received even a small part of the
glory due Him. *The heavens* declare the glory of God,
and *the earth* is full of His beauty, *but man* for the most
part, has not directed much glory to Him.

PART I — GOD'S GLORY DISTORTED
THROUGHOUT HISTORY

It was very risky indeed for God to create a being with *free will.* On the one hand, such a being could appreciate God's greatness, beauty, wisdom and love. On the other hand, he was free to go his own way, to ignore God and even to go against God's desires. Even beyond this, God allowed His arch enemy Satan free access to tempt, cajole and entice this being (and all his descendants) in the opposite direction, away from God's plan, that he might debase God's glory. Thus we can see that it was *extremely perilous* for God to take this route in His creation. What if *some* of these people He made actually did turn away and dishonor Him, rather than contributing to His glory?

This of course is precisely what took place! Only it wasn't just "some." *All* of them, every last one, "sinned and came short of the glory of God." (Rom. 3:23) In fact just before Paul made this statement he quoted these words from several painful and disheartening Old Testament passages: "There is no one righteous, not even one ...all have turned away; they have together become worthless; there is no one who does good, not even one. ...There is no fear of God before their eyes." (Rom. 3:10-18)

This is a mighty discouraging track record for man's presentation of God's magnificence. Truly God's glory has been a very fragile commodity in the hands of His highest creatures on earth. In fact, His glory was trampled in the dust by most of them.

PART II – A FEW HIGH POINTS IN HISTORY

Now we want to shift gears and go back to view a few encouraging incidents in Old Testament history. These must have been very pleasing to the Lord.

There were some brief periods when God's people saw His hand do mighty things, and they rose up to glorify Him. One of these times was immediately after their deliverance from Egypt when they had crossed the Red Sea and Pharaoh's army had drowned in the receding waters. (see Exodus 15:1-13)

Then, when David was king of Israel, the psalms he wrote are like mountain peaks rising out of a long, desolate plateau. We will be referring to these again further on. Additional rather short-lived bright spots were Solomon's dedication of his new temple, Elijah's victory over the prophets of Baal on Mt. Carmel, and the short revivals under Kings Hezekiah and Josiah. But probably the most notable high points from the standpoint of missions or outreach to the lost, are some of the responses to God's goodness on the part of the heathen.

One of these was Jethro, Moses' father-in-law, a pagan priest. He was greatly moved by the Lord's magnificent deliverance of His people Israel from Egypt. "Then Jethro rejoiced for all the good which the Lord had done for Israel, whom He had delivered out of the hand of the Egyptians. And Jethro said …'*Now I know that the Lord is greater than all the gods.'*" (Ex. 18:9-11)

Another was Rahab the prostitute of Jericho, who had heard about how the Lord had opened up the Red Sea for His people to cross over on dry land. She said to the spies Joshua had sent, "The Lord your God, he is God in heaven above, and on earth beneath." (Josh. 2:11)

Then there was Ruth the Moabite girl who had married Naomi's son. After Naomi's husband and both of her sons had died, she decided to return to her home in Bethlehem, but urged her daughters-in-law to remain in Moab because she was entirely destitute. However, Naomi's life had made such an impact on Ruth that she replied: "Entreat me not to leave you, or to turn back from following after you; for wherever you go, I will go; and wherever you lodge, I will lodge. Your people shall be my people, and your God, my God. Where you die, I will die, and there I will be buried." (Ruth 1:16,17) This was a high-point indeed for the glory of the Lord.

The book of Daniel contains several exaltations of God's worthiness, spoken by the heathen kings of Babylon, because of what the Lord did through Daniel when he was a captive in a foreign land. After God gave to Daniel the interpretation of King Nebuchadnezzar's dream, that great monarch replied, "Truly your God is the God of gods, the Lord of kings." And after God had protected His three Israelite witnesses in the fiery furnace, the king again declared, "There is no other God who can deliver like this." Then a third time, after God had healed his insanity, this same king declared, "Now I, Nebuchadnezzar, praise and extol and honor the King of heaven, all of whose works are truth, and His ways justice." (Dan. 4:37)

Some years later when Darius, a later king, had Daniel cast into the lions' den and God miraculously delivered him, the emperor sent out a mandate to his entire empire: "I make a decree that in every dominion of my kingdom men must tremble and fear before the God of Daniel. For He is the living God, and steadfast forever. His kingdom is the one which shall endure to the end. He delivers and rescues, and He works signs and wonders in heaven and on earth, Who has delivered Daniel from the power of the lions." (Dan. 6:26,27)

Now we move on to the amazing response of the people of Nineveh after Jonah preached judgment to them. "The people of Nineveh believed God, proclaimed a fast and put on sackcloth, from the greatest to the least of them. Then word came to the king of Nineveh, and he arose from his throne and laid aside his robe, covered himself with sackcloth and sat in ashes. And he caused it to be proclaimed and published throughout Nineveh by the decree of the king and his nobles saying, 'Let neither man nor beast, herd nor flock, taste anything; do not let them eat, or drink water. But let man and beast be covered with sackcloth and cry mightily to God. Yes, let everyone turn from his evil way and from the violence that is in his hands. Who can tell if God will turn and relent, and turn away from His fierce anger, so that we may not perish.' Then God saw their works, that they turned from their evil way, and God relented from the disaster that He had said He would bring upon them, and He did not do it." (Jonah 3:5-10)

There is also a touching remark about the impact of the gospel upon the people of Thesalonica in the New Testament. We can almost feel Paul's joy as he makes the statement: "You turned to God from idols to serve the living and true God." (I Thess. 1:9)

Truly it is a superb thrill to our heavenly Father when a pagan man gets his eyes opened to see the grandeur and splendor of our God, and begins to glorify Him. Surely this same fervor of excitement should become a driving motivation for each of us, His children.

PART III – VISIONS OF GOD'S WORLDWIDE GLORY IN THE SCRIPTURES

In this section we want to note that often God's glory is coupled with a desire for the world's various people groups to appreciate Him and all He offers. To put it simply, let us observe how frequently missions is related to God's glory in scripture.

In the Old Testament, the master worshipper was David, the man after God's own heart. Although David was not a missionary, he certainly had a heart for God's glory and longed for all mankind to know God and "ascribe unto the Lord the glory due to His name. (Ps. 29:2) Below, we will show a sampling from the Psalms of how David's missionary passion is linked to his worship.

"I will praise You, O Lord, *among the peoples.* I will sing to You *among the nations."* *Ps. 57:9; 108:3*

"O clap your hands, *all you peoples!* Shout to God with the voice of triumph! For the Lord most high is awesome; He is a great King over all the earth. Ps. 45:1,2

"God be merciful to us and bless us, and cause His face to shine upon us, *that Your way may be known on earth,* Your salvation *among all nations.* Let the peoples praise You, O God; *let all the peoples praise You."* Ps. 67:1-3

"Among the gods there is none like You, O Lord, nor are there any works like Your works. *All nations* whom You have made shall come and worship before You, O Lord, and shall glorify Your name, for You are great and do wondrous things. You alone are God." Ps. 86:8-10

"O sing to the Lord a new song! Sing to the Lord, *all the earth.* Sing to the Lord, bless His name. *Proclaim the good news of His salvation* from day to day. *Declare His glory among the nations, His wonders among all peoples."* For the Lord is great and greatly to be praised. He is to be feared above all gods, for all the gods of the peoples are idols. But the Lord made the heavens. Honor and majesty are before Him. Strength and beauty are in His sanctuary. Give to the Lord, *O families of the peoples,* give to the Lord glory and strength. Give to the Lord the glory due His name. Bring an offering and come into His courts. O worship the Lord in the beauty of holiness! Tremble before Him *all the earth.* Ps. 96:-1-9

"Praise the Lord, *all you Gentiles!* Laud Him, *all you peoples!* For His merciful kindness is great toward us, and the truth of the Lord endures forever. Praise the Lord!" Ps. 117:1,2

Although David was an Israelite and loved his nation, especially its capital city of Zion, he still wished for all the other families of the earth to share the blessing of knowing his God. David was certainly no Pharisee, nor was he a racist.

Another great prophet who had visions of God's grandeur and majesty was Isaiah. Let us examine God's call to him and God's final revelation to him.

"In the year that King Uzziah died, I saw the Lord sitting on a throne, high and lifted up, and the train of His robe filled the temple. ...And the posts of the door were shaken by the voice of him who cried out, and the house was filled with smoke. ...Also I heard the voice of the Lord saying,

'Whom shall I *send*, and who will *go* for Us?' Then I said, 'Here am I! *Send me!*'" (Is. 6:1-8)

In the final chapter of Isaiah's book, we hear the Lord saying, "It shall be that I will gather *all nations and tongues;* and they shall come and see My glory. ...And they shall declare My glory *among the Gentiles.*" (Is. 66:18,19)

Now we skip to the last book of the Old Testament, and we hear the prophet Malachi also sharing with us a beautiful word from the Lord regarding missions and God's glory.

"From the rising of the sun, even to its going down, My name shall be great *among the Gentiles. In every place* incense shall be offered to My name, and a pure offering. For 'My name shall be great *among the nations' says the Lord of hosts.*" Mal. 1:11

When we turn to the New Testament, we find missions linked even closer to the glory of God. Six months before the Lord Jesus' birth, when John the Baptist's father Zacharias gave his great prophecy of praise for the coming Savior, he concluded with these words: "to give light to those who sit in darkness and the shadow of death." Then on that first Christmas eve when the angel announced the Savior's birth, he said, "Behold, I bring you good tidings of great joy which shall be *to all people.* ...And then "Suddenly a great company of the heavenly host appeared with the angel, *praising God and saying, 'Glory to God in the highest...'*" (Lk. 2:10,13,14)

Paul's missionary call came as a follow-up to his blinding vision of the glory of the resurrected Christ. Note how he relates it.

"Since I could not see for the glory of that light, being led by the hand of those who were with me, I came to Damascus. Then a certain Ananias, a devout man according to the law, having a good testimony with all the Jews who dwelt there, came to me; and he stood and said to me, 'Brother Saul, receive your sight.' And at that same hour I looked at him. Then he said, 'The God of our fathers has chosen you that you should know His will, and see the Just One, and hear the voice of His mouth. For *you will be His witness to all men* of what you have seen and heard.' ...Then He said to me, 'Depart, for I will send you far from here *to the Gentiles.'*" Acts 22:11-21

And it is really quite moving to look at a sample of what he wrote to both the Jews and the Gentiles in Rome:

"I tell you that Christ has become a servant of the Jews on behalf of God's truth, to confirm the promises made to the patriarchs *so that the Gentiles may glorify God for His mercy,* as it is written: 'Therefore *I will praise you among the Gentiles; I will sing hymns to your name.'* Again, it says, *'Rejoice, O Gentiles with His people.'* And again, *'Praise the Lord all you Gentiles, and sing praises to Him, all you peoples.'*" (Rom. 15:8-11)

Now let us notice what he wrote to the Gentiles at Ephesus:

"Praise be to the God and Father of our Lord Jesus Christ, who has blessed us in the heavenly realms with every spiritual blessing in Christ, *...to the praise of His glorious grace...* In Him we were chosen ... *in order that we,* who were the first to hope in Christ, *might be for the praise of His glory. And you also were included in Christ when you heard the word of truth, the gospel of your salvation ... to the praise of His glory."* (Eph. 1:3-14)

As mentioned earlier, in the book of Revelation the apostle John saw two

visions of throngs of angels and other beings from earth and heaven gathered around God's throne. Let us look closely at who were included in those multitudes as they worshipped Him and the Lamb:

"And they sang a new song, saying: 'You are worthy to take the scroll, and to open its seals, for You were slain, and have redeemed us to God by Your blood *out of every tribe and tongue and people and nation.'*" Rev. 5:9,10

"I looked, and behold, a great multitude which no one could number, *of all nations, tribes, peoples, and tongues,* standing before the throne and before the Lamb, clothed with white robes, with palm branches in their hands, and crying out with a loud voice, saying: 'Salvation belongs to our God Who sits on the throne, and to the Lamb.'" Rev. 7:9,10

Yes, missions has a great deal to do with God's glory.

PART IV – GOD'S GLORY IN THE WORLD TODAY

There is certainly no even distribution of those who worship the true and living God throughout the world today. In fact, there is a painful disparity. I have lived in the Los Angeles area many years of my life, but I have also spent a long time in various regions of Asia. In Los Angeles and its surroundings, there are literally thousands of churches, and most of these are good, solid groups of believers who sincerely worship the Lord in spirit and truth. A number of these congregations have well over a thousand in attendance on a Sunday morning, even dividing into two or three services.

In Asia things are very different. In Japan for example, few of the scattered churches have an attendance of more than a dozen or two. India now has almost a billion people, and much of that nation is only about 0.1% Christian. All the rest give their worship to false gods, for they do not know the true God. North Korea has known no visible church life for fifty years. The whole Russian empire suffered for decades under the heavy pressure of atheism, and even most of Europe has languished under the weight of materialism. Thus the picture of God's glory in the world today is certainly one of inequality and imbalance. These facts should constitute a strong appeal for missions.

CHAPTER 8

Seize the Baton!

Since this will be the last chapter of this book, we will turn our attention to some specific suggestions. However, from the outset let me repeat again that there are different ways of being involved in missions. A missionary challenge should never result in a guilt trip. Our service for the Lord should be joyously and freely given. Otherwise it is highly questionable whether we have a clear comprehension of what He is asking us to do. I have seen a number of people go through the rigorous proceedings to become a missionary, only to wash out and return home after a difficult, frustrating attempt.

As we have mentioned before, not all Christians are called to go overseas to some unreached people group. In fact, for every one who is sent out by the Lord, a large number of supporting Christians here at home are needed to keep him effective in his work. Let us give some thought, then, to the various roles which need to be filled.

Parents

We will begin with the element of parenting. If all Christian parents would round out the devotional training of their children with an emphasis on God's heart for missions, the entire world could be reached with a vital presentation of God's love within a generation or two.

There are various ways to share a vision for missions with children. One very effective means is to ask the Lord's blessing on a missionary or two each time the family gives thanks for food at the dinner table.

Another interesting and helpful family activity is to read aloud together some missionary biographies and also to watch the missionary videos now being produced for children. When missionaries speak at their church, inviting them home for a meal can give those missionaries a chance to build a first-hand relationship with the children of a family. Parents can also go with their children on missionary tours; what better way to spend a vacation? I know of some youngsters who have become so concerned for the needy children in another land that they are determined to share their toys with them, go shopping on their behalf, and start saving part of their own money to send to them.

Sunday School Teachers

Sunday School teachers are in a natural position to teach missions, since the Bible from beginning to end is a textbook on missions. Many churches have found it very helpful for their Sunday School teachers and other leaders to attend the "Perspectives" course which is taught by the U.S. Center for World Missions.*

*This organization has offices scattered throughout the U.S., and will send representatives to your church to teach the course. Their main address is: U.S.C.W.M.; 16-5 E. Elizabeth St.; Pasadena, CA. 91104-2721. Tel. 626 - 797- 1111. Or Email: perspectives@uscwm.org

Youth Workers

Small teams of young people going for a short term to help a resident missionary with his work on the field are becoming more and more popular. The results are often quite gratifying – to the young people themselves, to the missionaries, to the local people of the country, and even to the folks in the home church as the group returns and gives their enthusiastic report. There is no substitute for direct, hands-on experience!

For such efforts to be most effective, however, there needs to be adequate training, both before they leave the home church and after they arrive on the field, and regular evaluation sessions while they are there. Every aspect of the venture must be covered with earnest prayer. Some teams, after they arrive on the field, divide into two groups, taking turns going out to do their ministry while the other group stays at base camp to pray. The home church too should be enlisted to support them in prayer, with each young person having certain prayer partners committed to pray for him daily.

Pastors

It has been said that the pastor's degree of concern for missions will have the largest part in determining the missionary vision of the whole church. Even though the church may have a strong missions committee, its effectiveness is limited without the propelling drive of the pastor.. He is the one who puts together the sermon topics for the year. He invites outside speakers and is the one who basically determines the prevailing atmosphere and concerns of his people.

Financial supporters

Once we begin to have contact with missionary enterprises around the world, we soon become aware of the need, not only for personnel, but for considerable funding as well. What amazing doors are opening up these days for the spread of the gospel to the ends of the earth! It surely is not God's plan that His people should have to be urged or even begged to participate. We cannot all go in person, but we can each have a vital part in reaching the world with our faithful giving.

Here is the story of a young man I met some years ago at Park Street Church in Boston. As you may know, Park Street Church holds a huge week-long missions conference every year. Missionary booths fill the basement of the church, and after the evening service each night people gather in the basement to look over the exhibits and fellowship together.

One evening as I was visiting there with a friend, he introduced me to a young man about thirty years old who came walking by. After he had left my friend began to tell me about him. Some years before he had a strong desire to become a missionary, but a severe speech problem caused him to hesitate. So he sought out his pastor, Dr. Ockenga, about his concern. Dr. Ockenga advised him to seek the Lord for some other means by which he could become vitally involved in missionary outreach.

He began to pray about this, and one morning on his way to work he noticed a "for rent" sign in front of a small gas station. For the next few days he couldn't seem to get that little sign out of his mind. Finally he decided that the Lord wanted him to rent that small, insignificant gas station and start a mini-business. As he made arrangements to take it over, he asked the Lord to prosper his efforts so that he could not only meet his own needs, but earn enough to send out a young man to the mission field in his place.

God granted his request and within a year he was able to support a godly young man to take his place on a needy field. He then asked the Lord to prosper his business so that after another year he could send out a second missionary. And the Lord did so. At the time I met him five years later, he was supporting five new missionaries on the field!

As disciples of Jesus Christ, shouldn't each of us seek His pattern for our personal involvement in fulfilling His Great Commission? Then we need to organize and plan our giving in a systematic way so that we can give generously and not grudgingly. If we set aside a definite portion each month for missions, we can then meet challenges that come our way — not with reluctance but with excitement at being able to have a part in spreading the gospel "to the ends of the earth."

Since retiring from our work in Taiwan, I have been impressed with the fact that most Christians here in the United States drive a good car and live in a comfortable home. They can afford to have pets, hobbies, nice clothes, and give good care to their families. Therefore, making reasonable contributions to the Lord's world-wide missions enterprise should not be any great burden for most of them. In fact, some people have learned to live on a scale which allows them to contribute significantly to God's program for the world. And if a measure of extra trust in His provision is needed, God will honor such faith and will add special blessing to the one who joyously gives to spread His gospel!

Furlough Helpers

The usual term for a missionary on the field is three to five years, then he returns home for furlough. A mini-sabbatical of six months to a year is filled with an assortment of obligations and duties. Most mission boards now speak of this time as the missionary's "home assignment." The tasks expected of him during this home break include physical checkups plus any needed treatments, and visits and reports to each of his supporting churches and individual donors. Study courses are often recommended, and of course a period of debriefing at his mission headquarters. Times of reunion with various family members and also some vacation and periods of R & R need to be worked in.

Two very important items will be needed: a reliable car to drive, and an adequate house or apartment to stay in. The home church can take a tremendous load off the process of re-entry by actively helping to locate and obtain these two things. Then if one group in the church will "adopt" the missionary family for the furlough period, the mutual blessing afforded can be great. Including the missionary husband in a fishing trip or a football game or taking the wife along to find shopping bargains will be much appreciated. Inviting the family into your home for a meal, or taking the couple out to one of your favorite restaurants can be something very special.

The Sunday School could make sure the m.k.s are included in summer camp experiences. The youth groups can reach out and involve them in their various activities. The shortness of time does not allow for the usual gradual period of adjustment, and so sensitivity in these areas of practical living can greatly alleviate some of the pressures of furlough and deputation.

Outreach with JESUS Video

Today in the United States there are many pockets of unreached people from nations overseas. One very effective way of gaining a hearing for the gospel is by making a gift of the JESUS video in their own language. These videos are available by calling: 1 - (800) 432- 1997.

Prayer Supporters

Prayer is a baton we can all carry. Whether we ever step on foreign soil or not, we can become a Prayer Partner with some of those who go in person. And these days through Email we can even hear how the battle is going and stand right alongside those on the front lines, doing battle with them! Taking the gospel to the ends of the earth must be a team effort involving both those who send and those who go. Effective prayer backing is by far the missionary's most crucial need, and no missionary should go to the field without a group of Prayer Partners who are committed to faithfully stand with him as he goes.

A missionary is in essence entering enemy territory! Not that the people around him are necessarily hostile, but all unreached people groups are bound and blinded by unseen forces which are responsible for their spiritual darkness. And these demonic forces certainly do not welcome the missionary or his efforts to bring a liberating gospel. "For we wrestle not against flesh and blood, but against spiritual forces..." (Eph. 6: 12) and "The weapons of our warfare are not carnal, but mighty through God to the pulling down of strongholds." (II Cor. 10:4)

How can we set about to become an effective Prayer Supporter? Here are a few practical suggestions:

- Focus on a certain area of the world, and on specific missionaries you can pray for by name. (You will want to add names of their national co-workers as well as you learn of them.)

- Make a commitment to those missionaries to pray regularly for them and arrange ways for them to keep you informed and in touch with what God is doing.

- Make it your business to learn about the people and the situation they are working in.

- Begin a prayer notebook where you collect scripture verses and materials to help you in effective praying.

Another helpful way to pray focuses on groups of unreached people rather than on any missionary you have met in person. If you are just getting started in praying for missions, or even if this has been your ministry for some time, I strongly suggest that you subscribe to the Global Prayer Digest. It is a little monthly magazine which will introduce you to some of the unreached or very needy mission fields. On a daily basis, along with interesting stories and illustrations, it will give you many ideas on how to pray for those people. I have used this material for a couple of years now and find it helpful and informative. Also their monthly magazine Mission Frontiers contains reports on the latest developments in the overall work of missions.

*You can order the Global Prayer Digest or Mission Frontiers from: U.S. Center for World Missions; 1605 Elizabeth St., Pasadena, CA; 91104. Or call by phone: (626) 398-2249. Email: subscriptions@global-prayer-digest.org

My challenge to every reader is this: whatever your involvement in God's program of missions, give it high priority. SEIZE THE BATON FIRMLY! Be assured that the eternal welfare of 8,000 people groups still unreached — the glory of God Himself — and your own joy of accomplishment — are all bound up with you as you help get the gospel to the unreached regions of our world!